These 50 images and extra blank spaces are for you to color, doodle, jot down your ideas, ANYTHING you want! Add your own special style and make these pages your own. Most importantly, have fun!

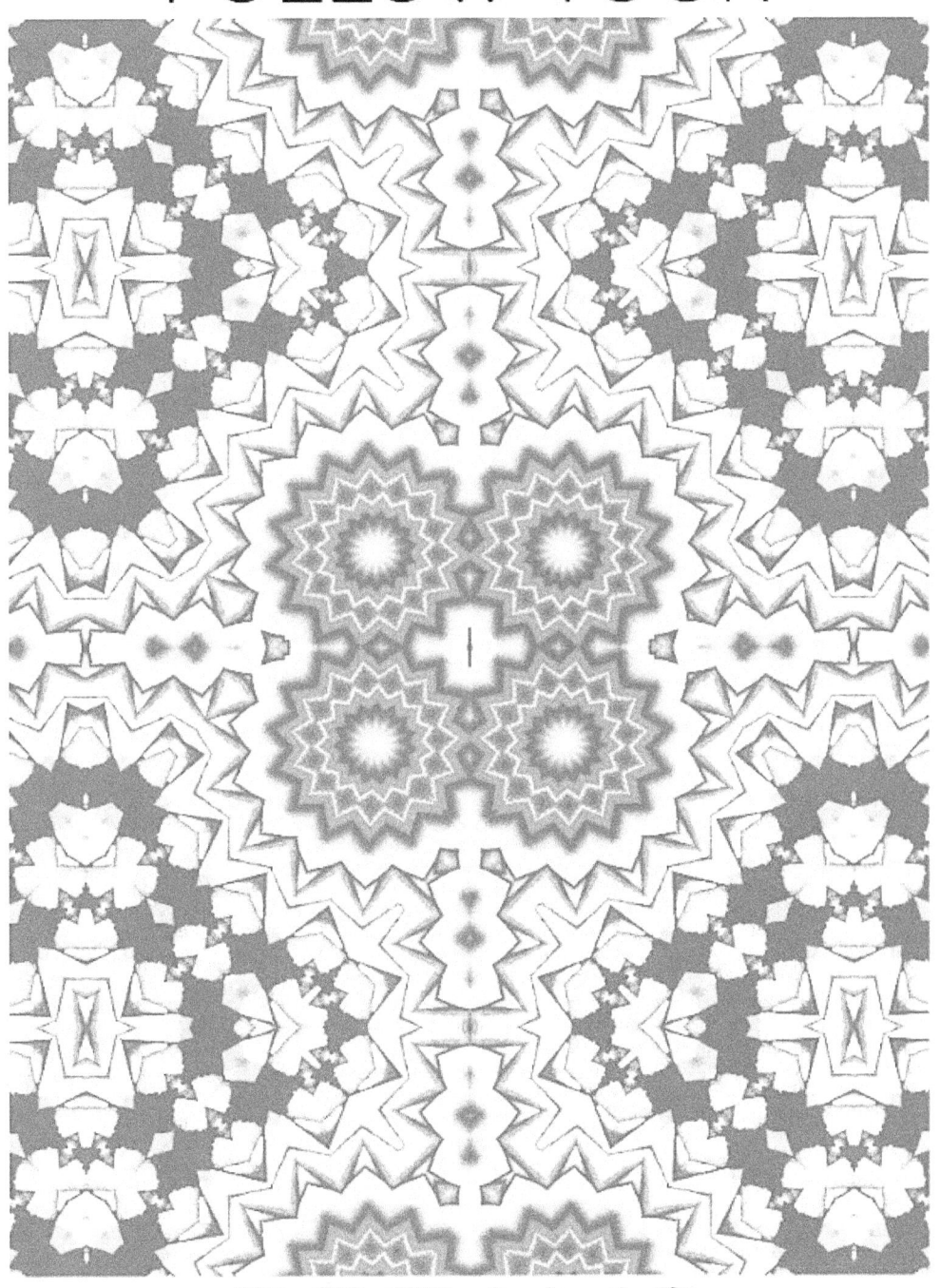

TRANQUILITY EXISTS

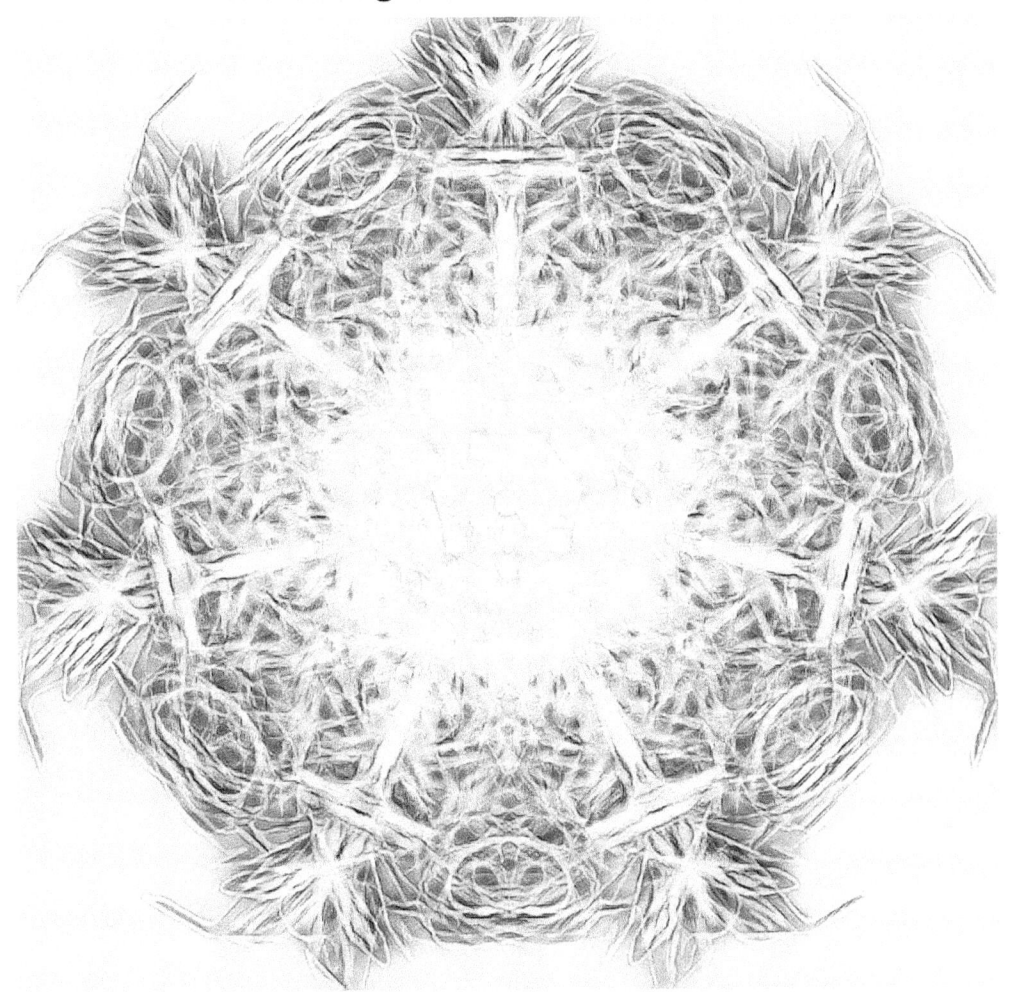

WITHIN YOU

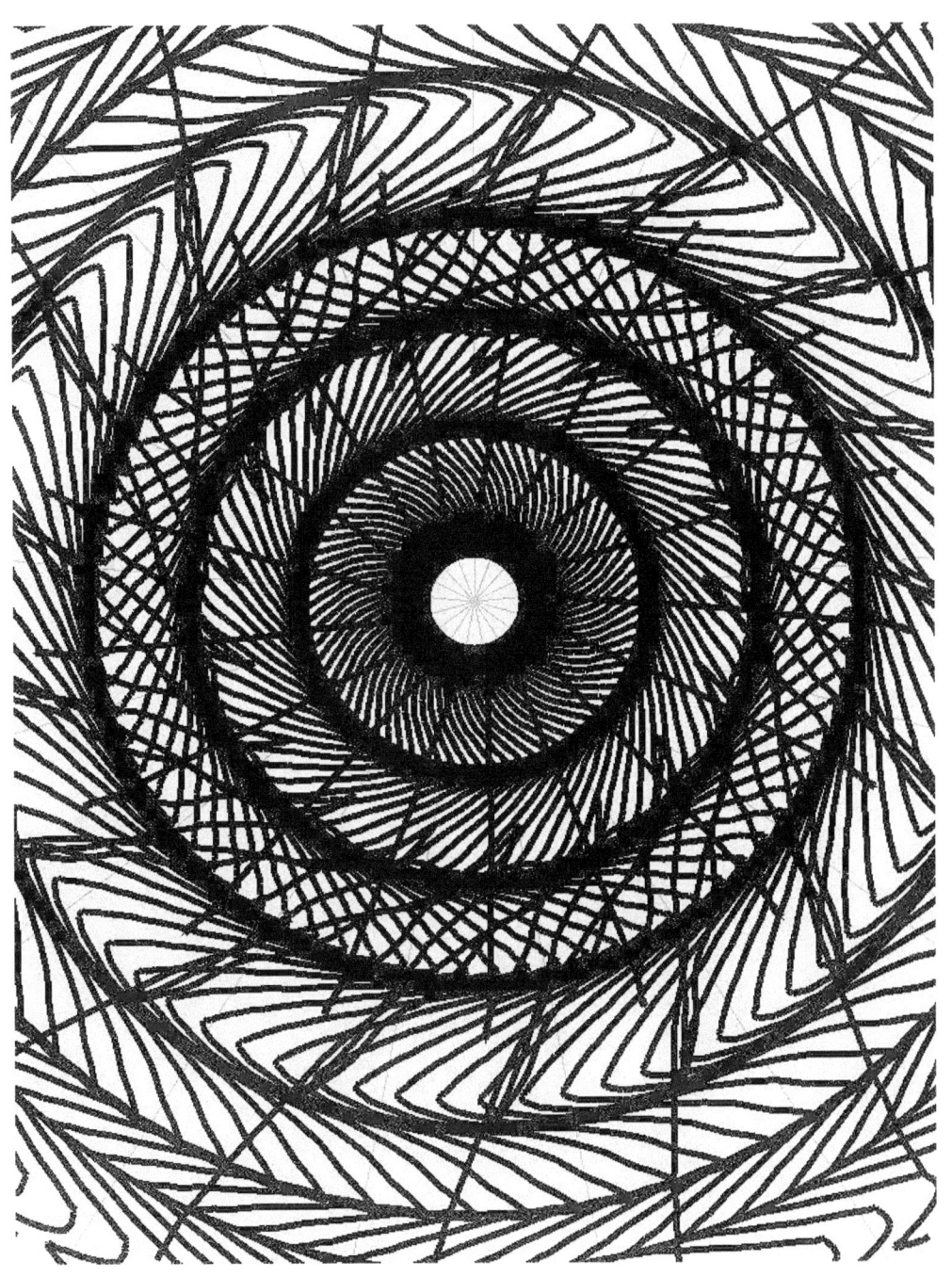

YOUR LIFE

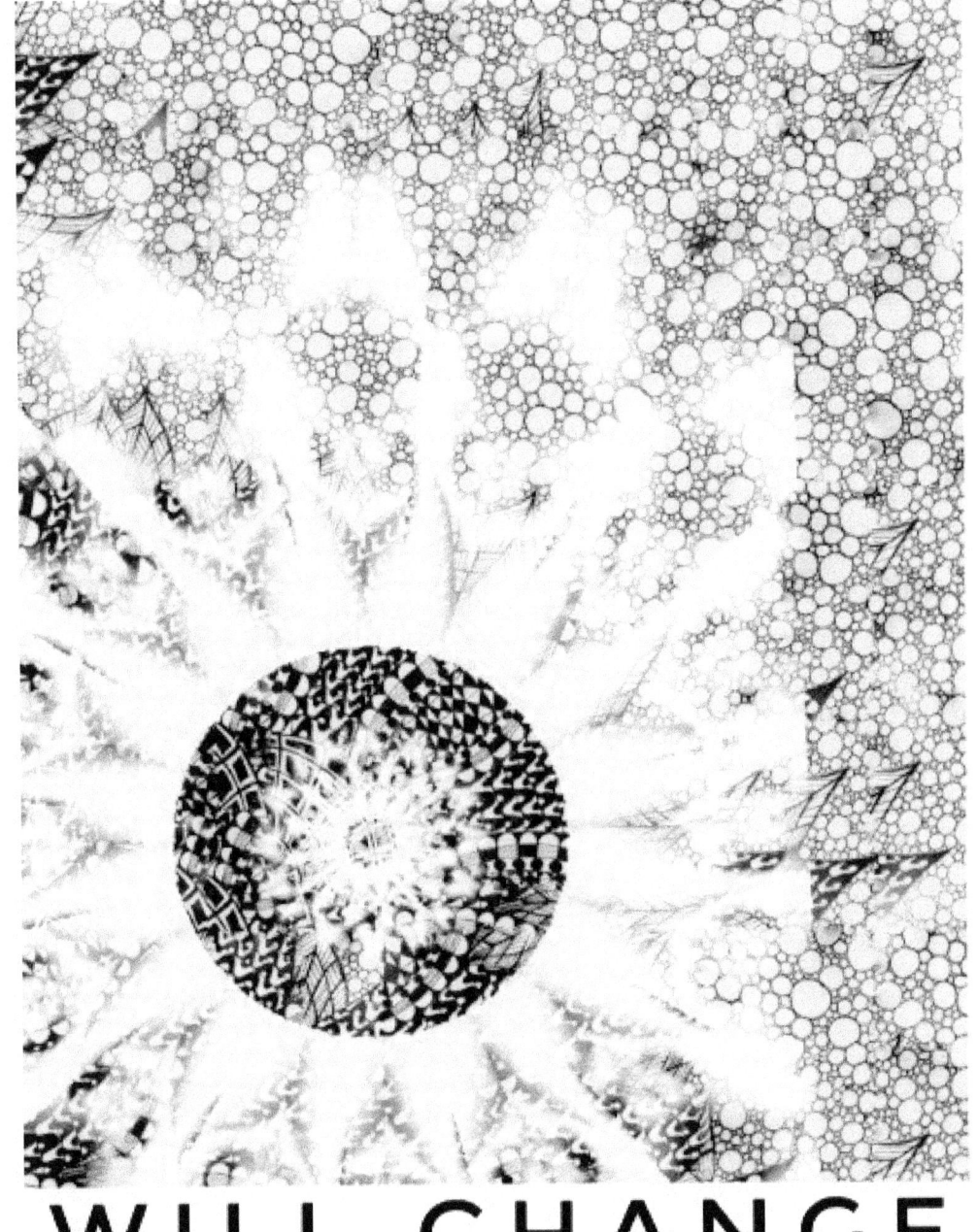

WILL CHANGE

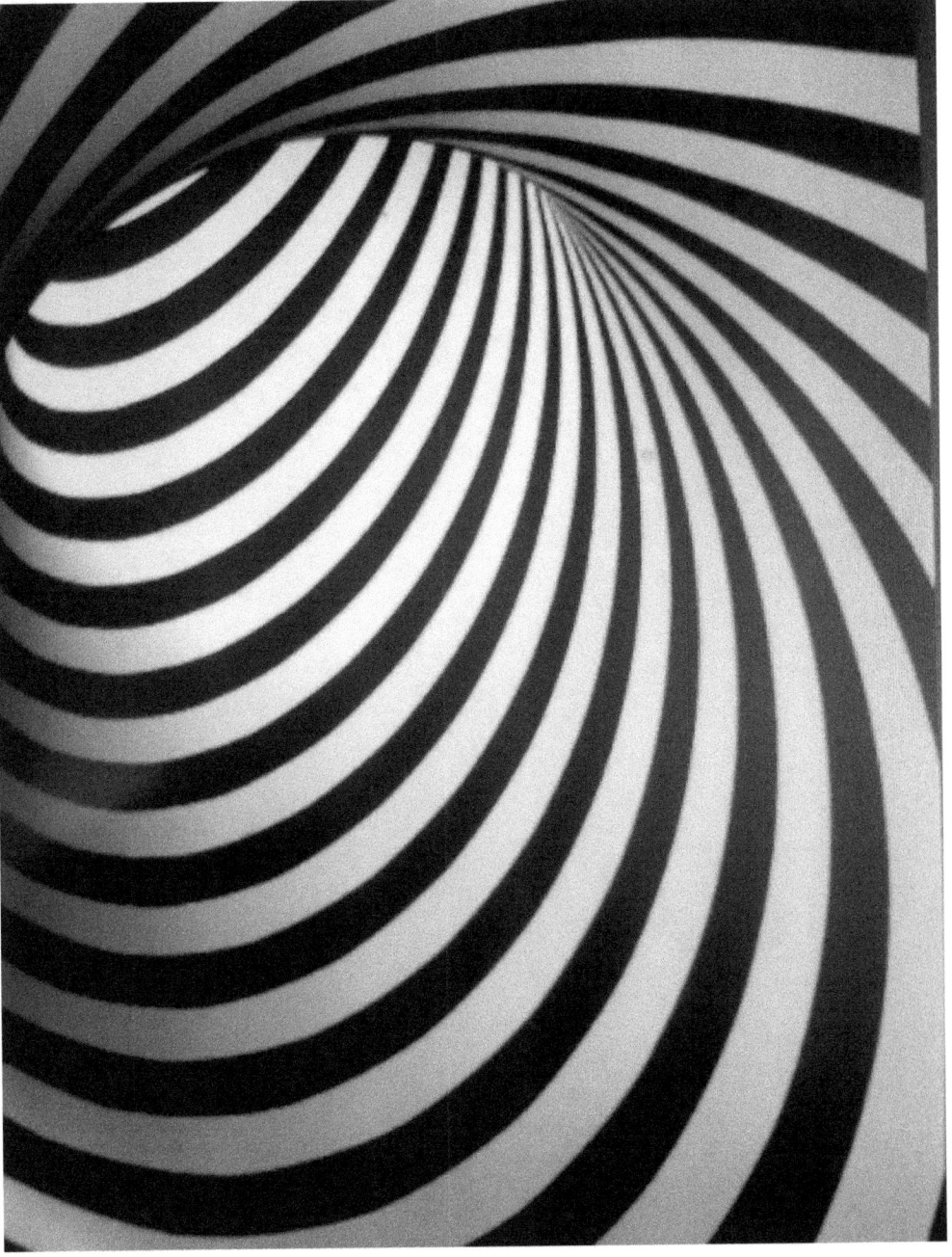

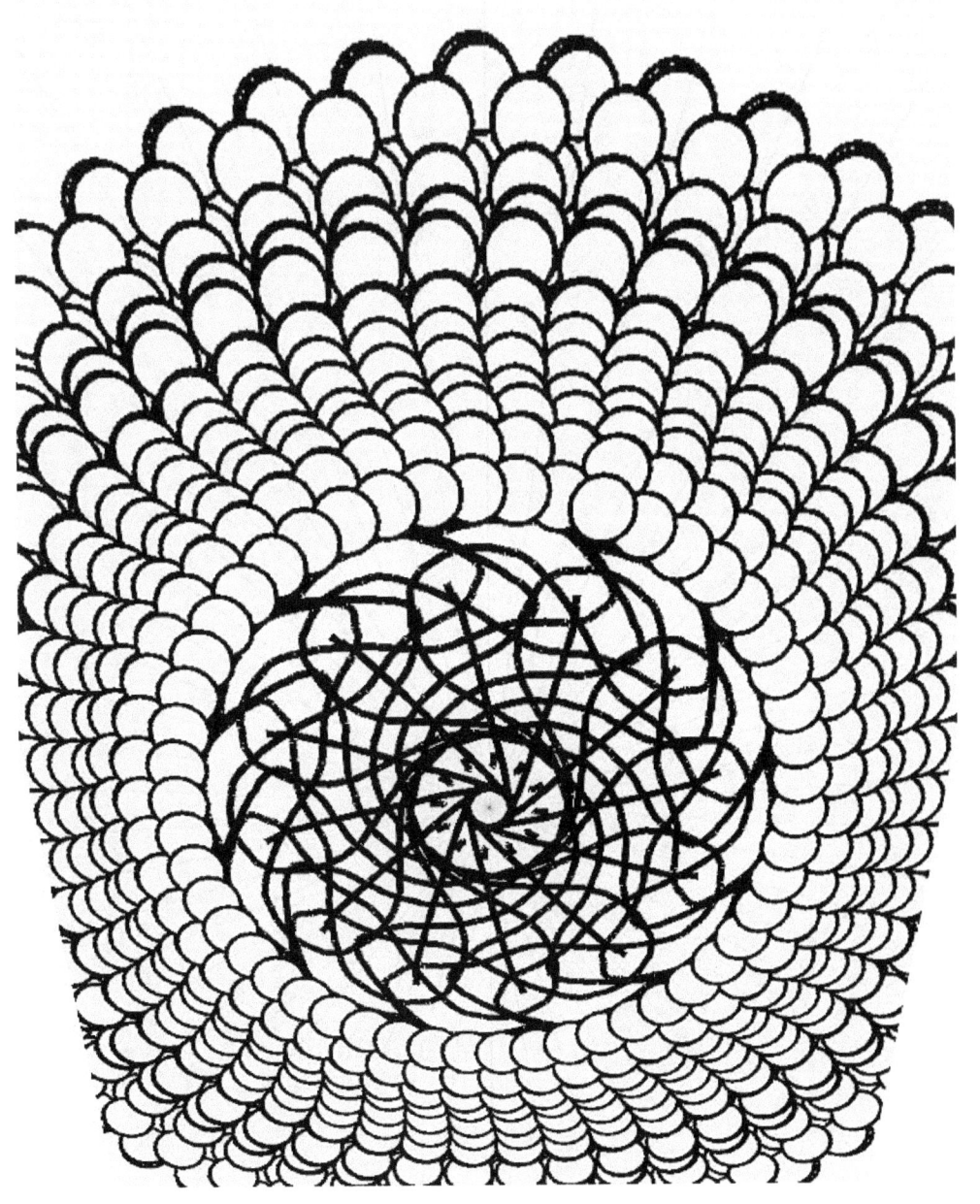

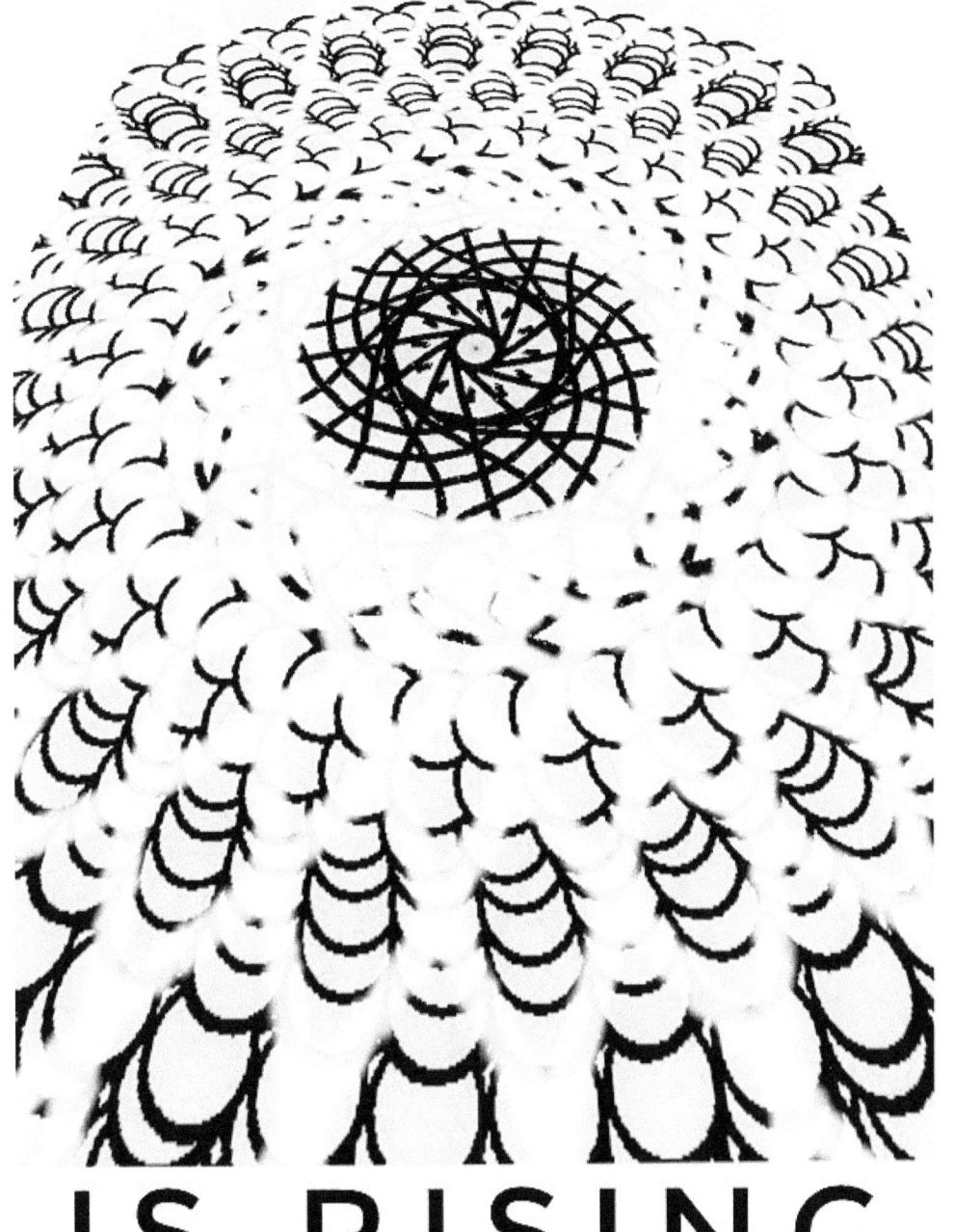

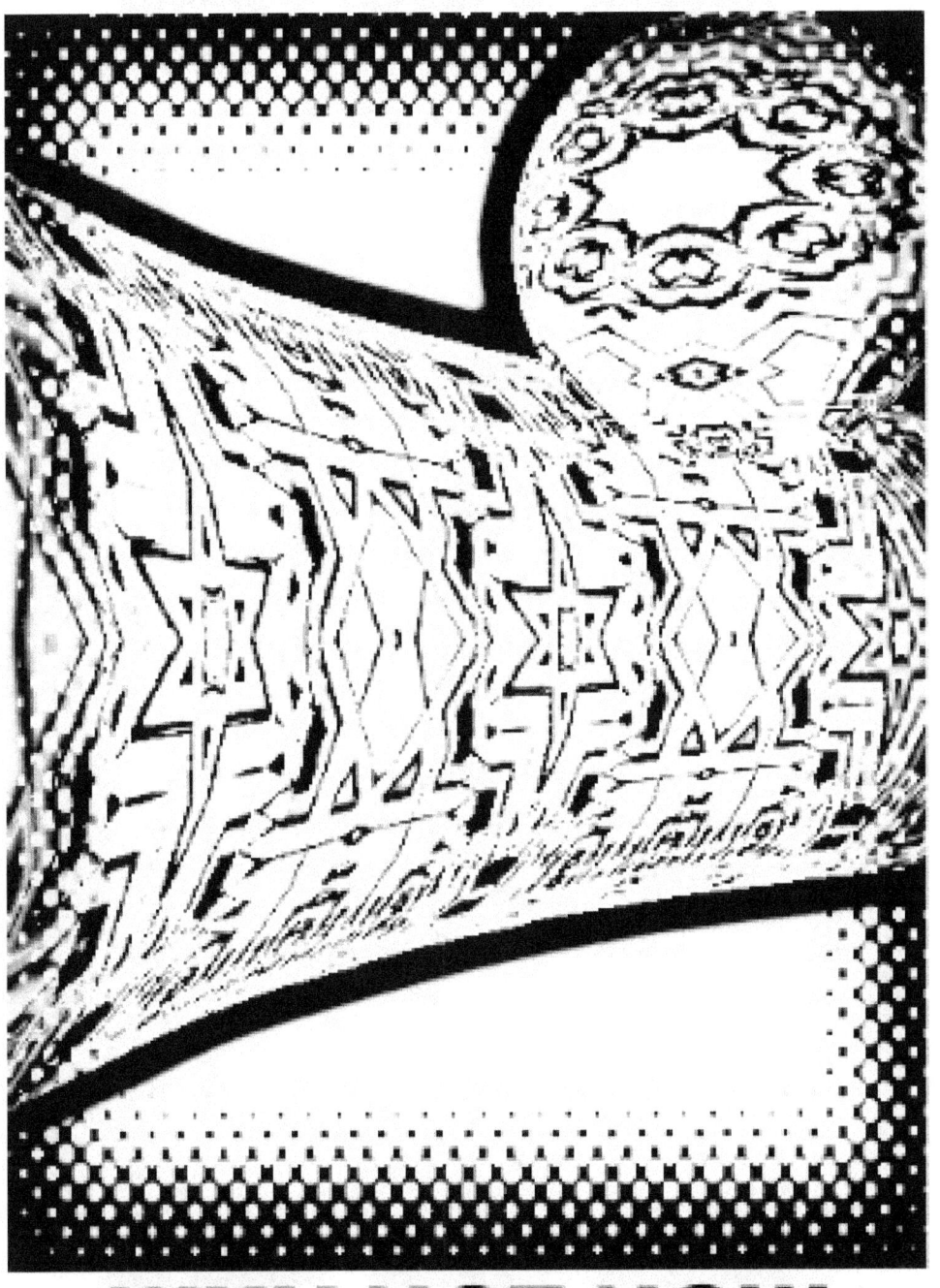

CHANGE IS

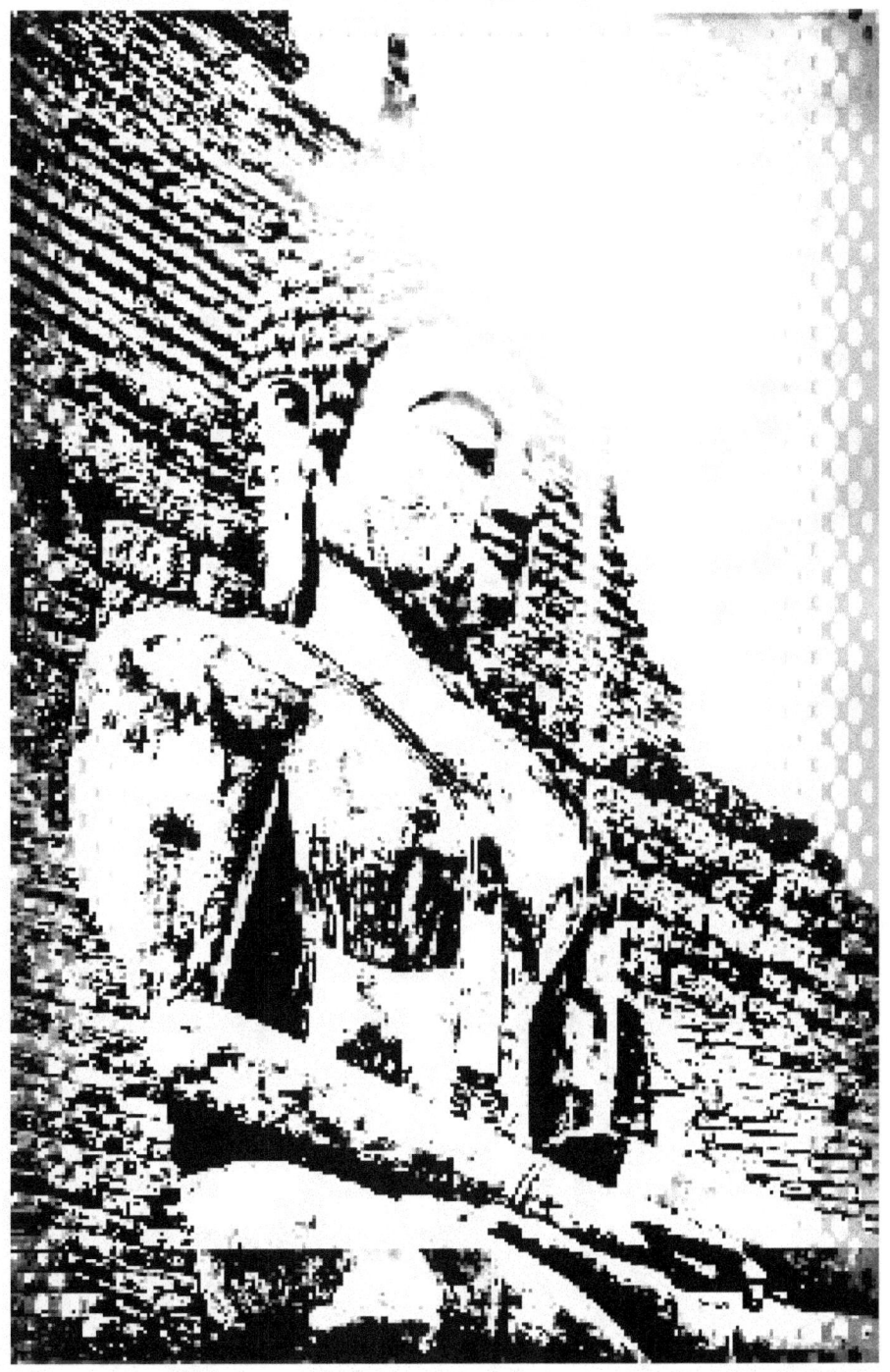

ONE MOMENT

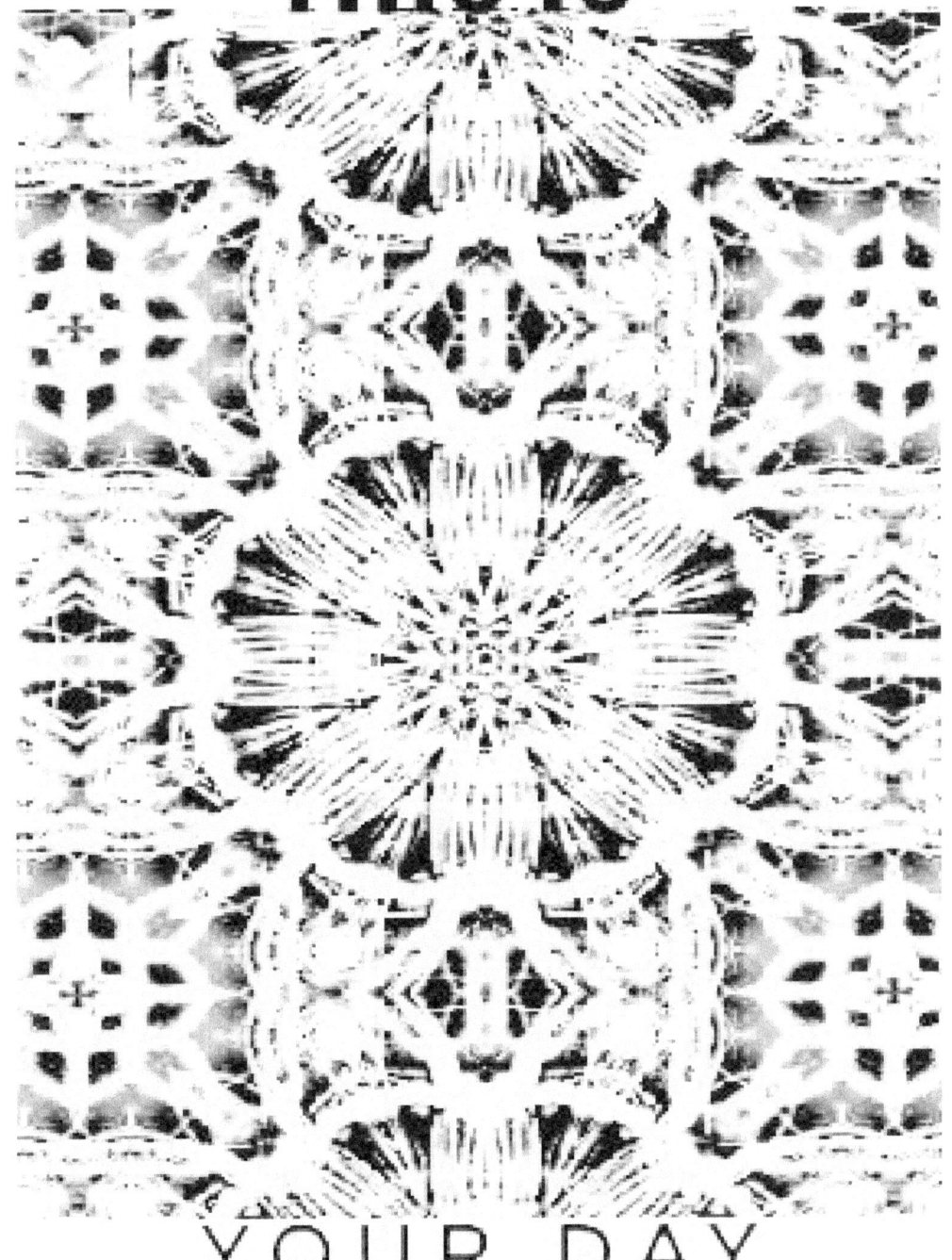

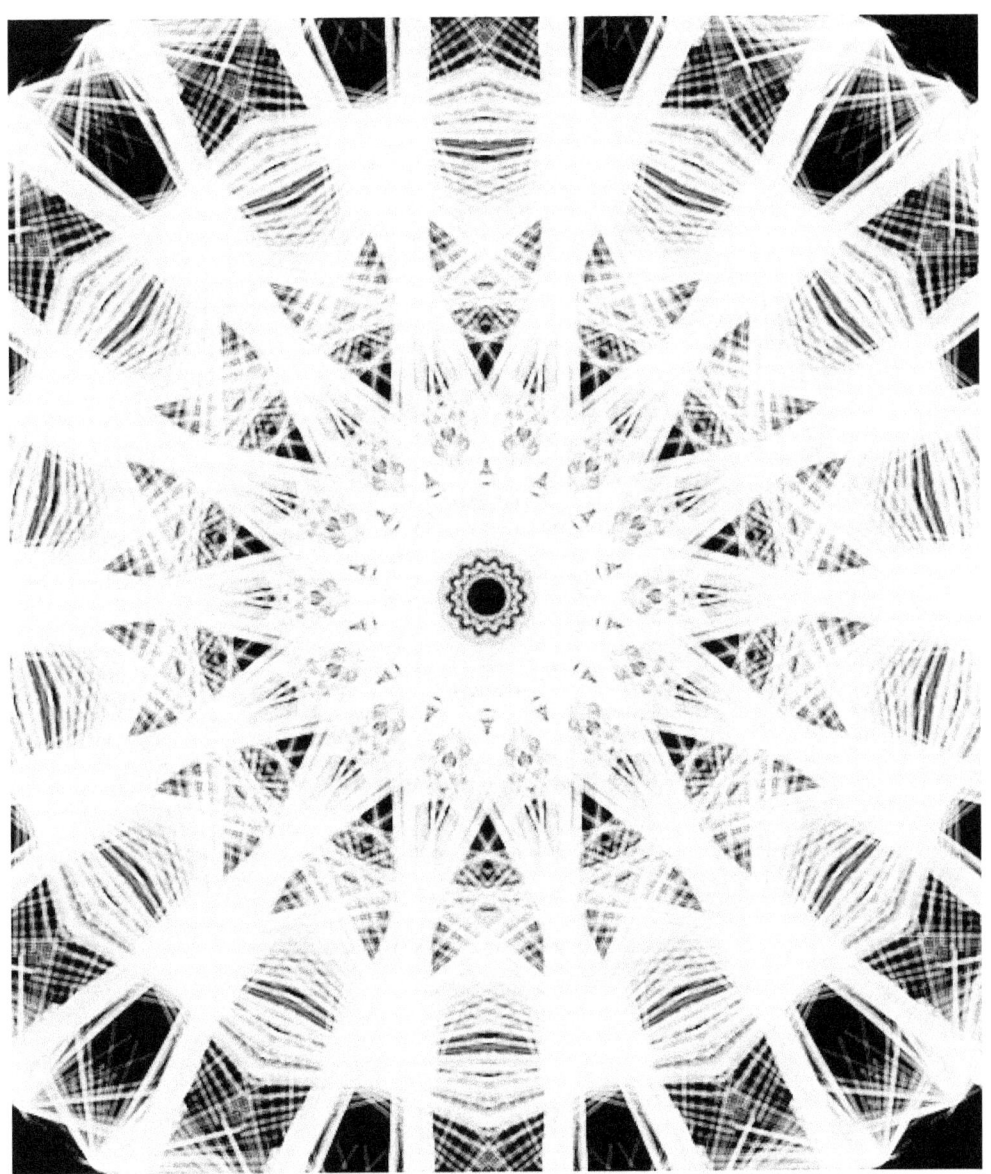

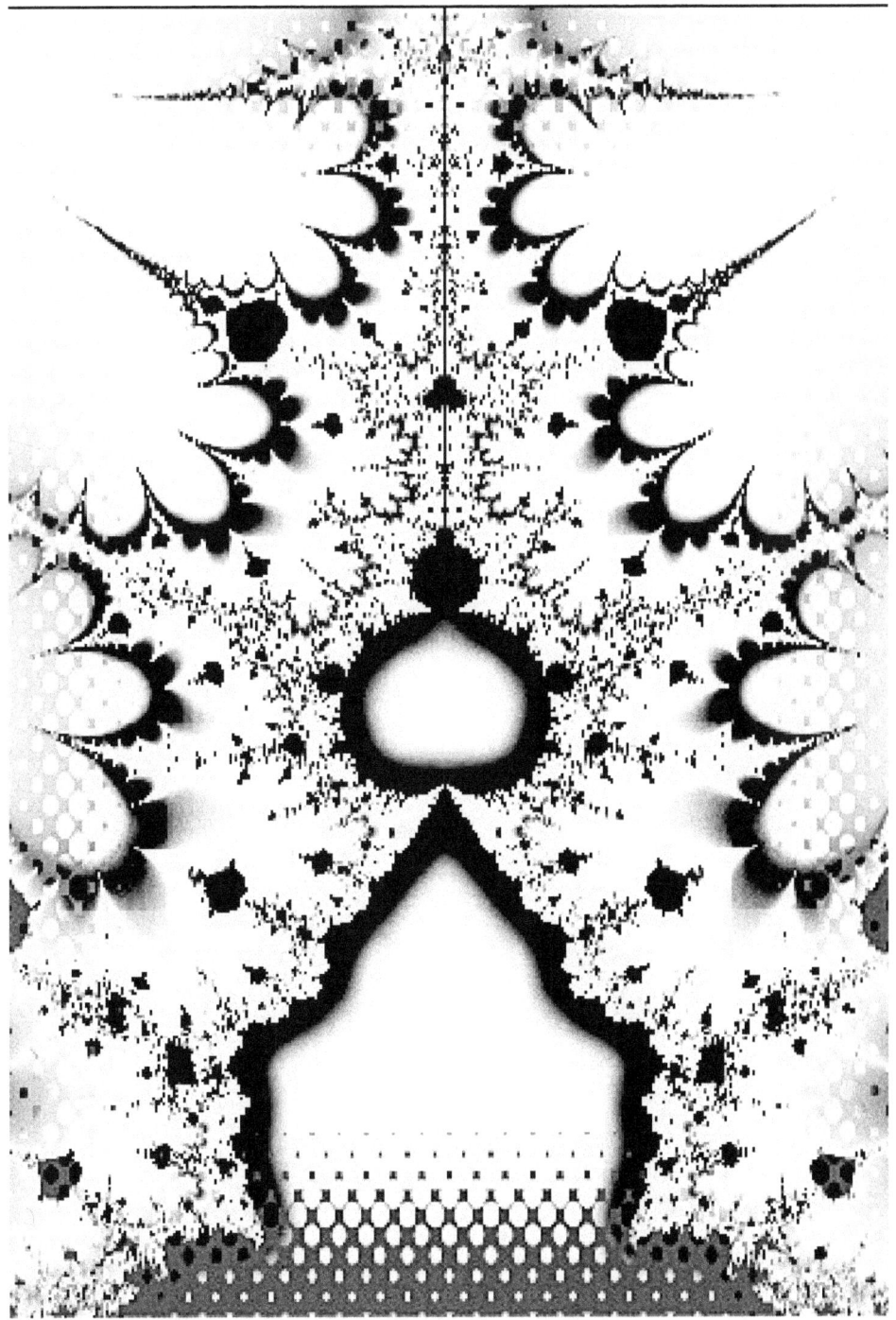

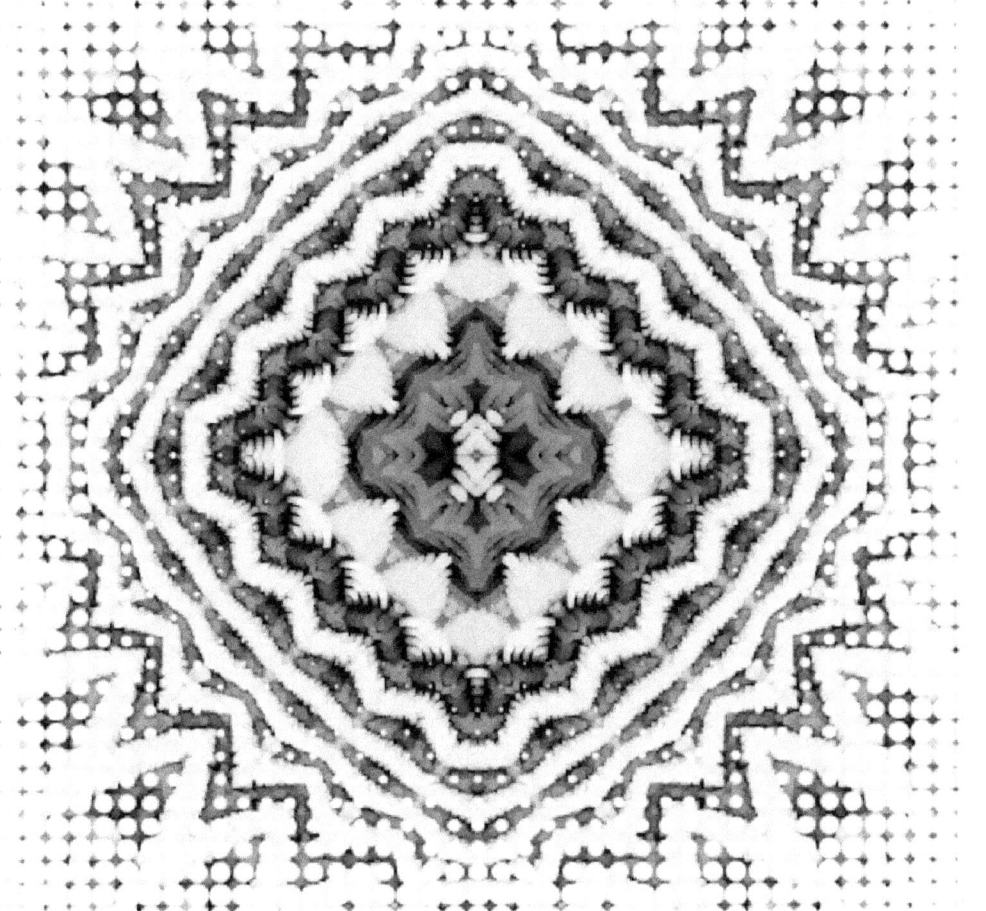

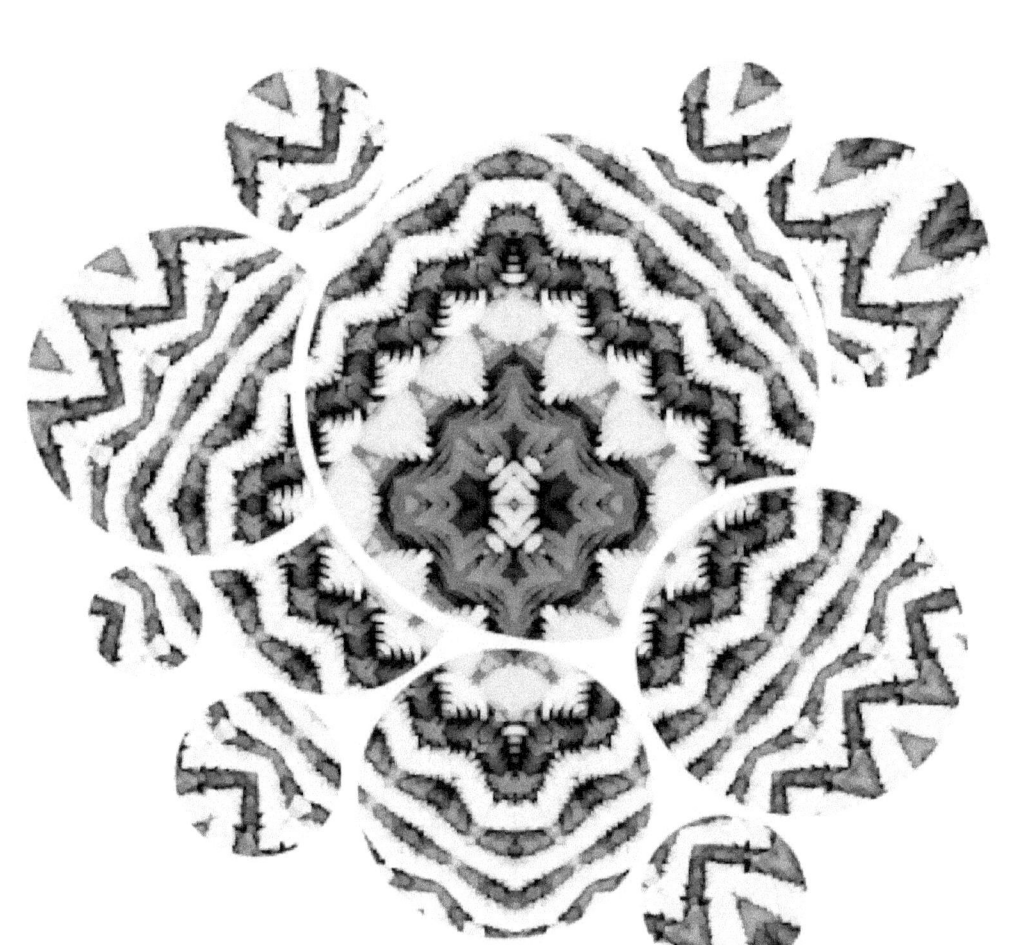

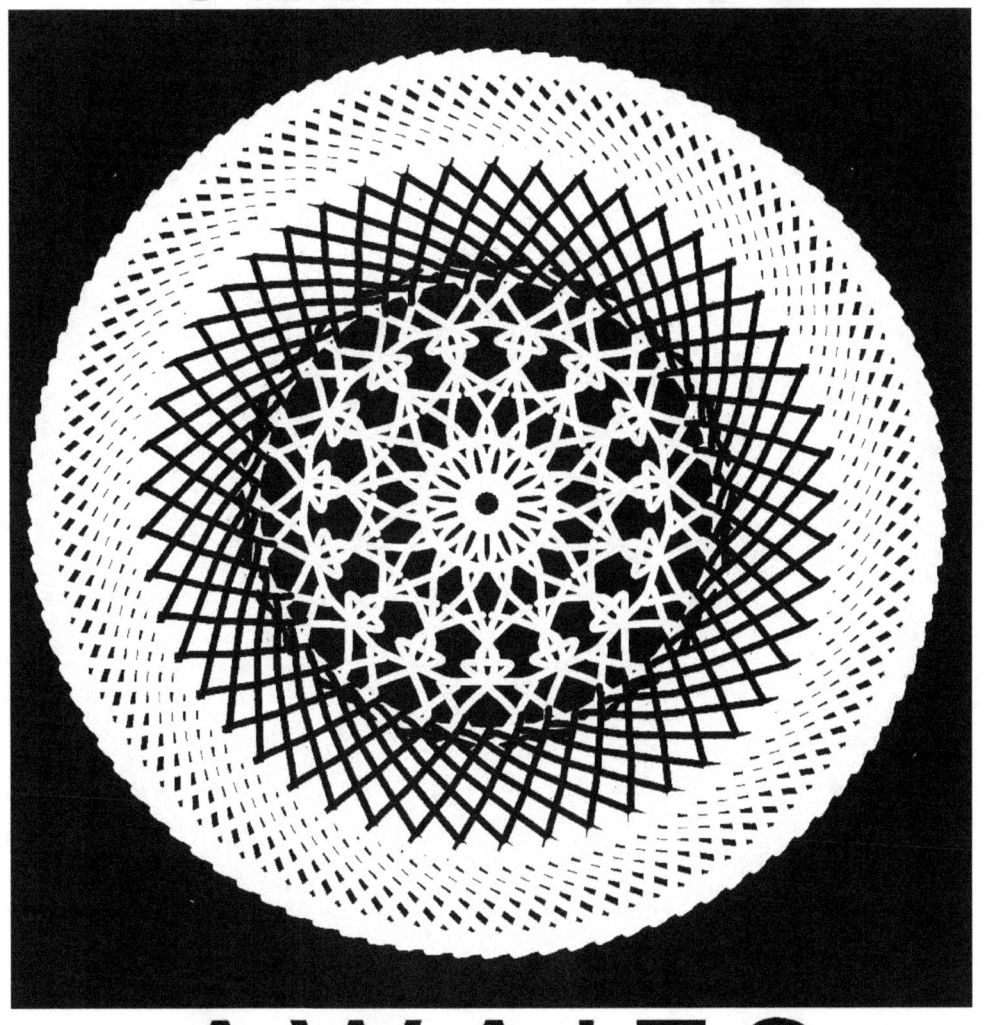

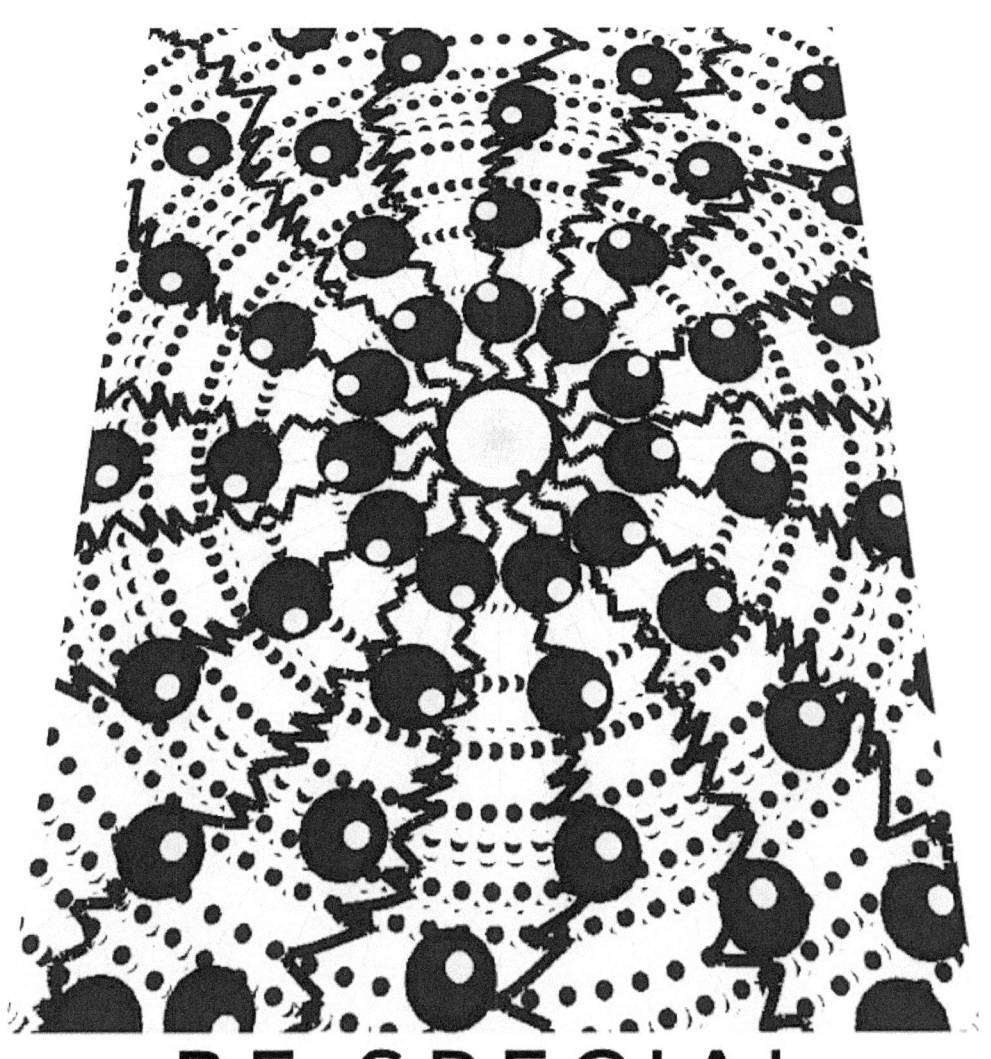

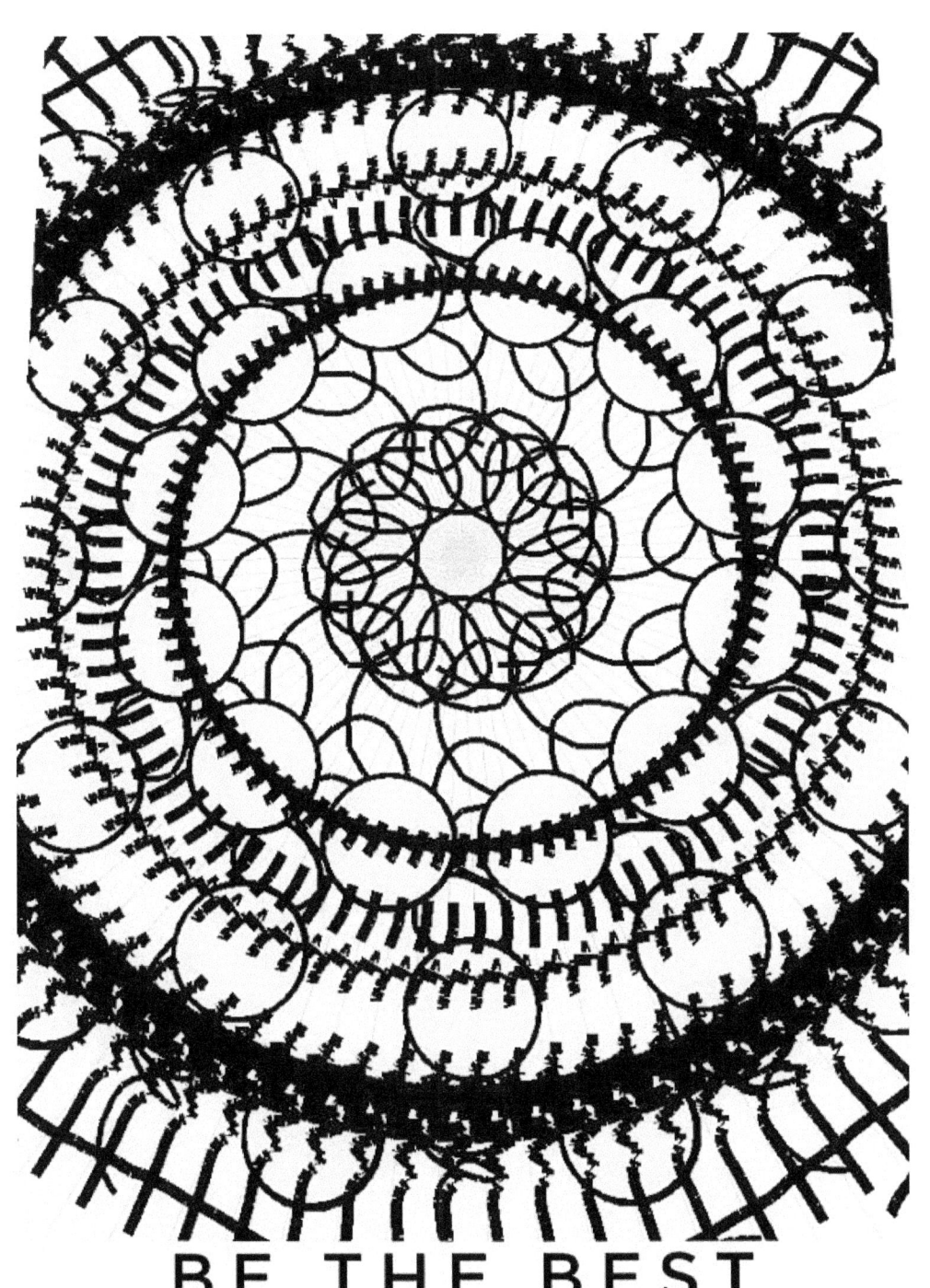
BE THE BEST

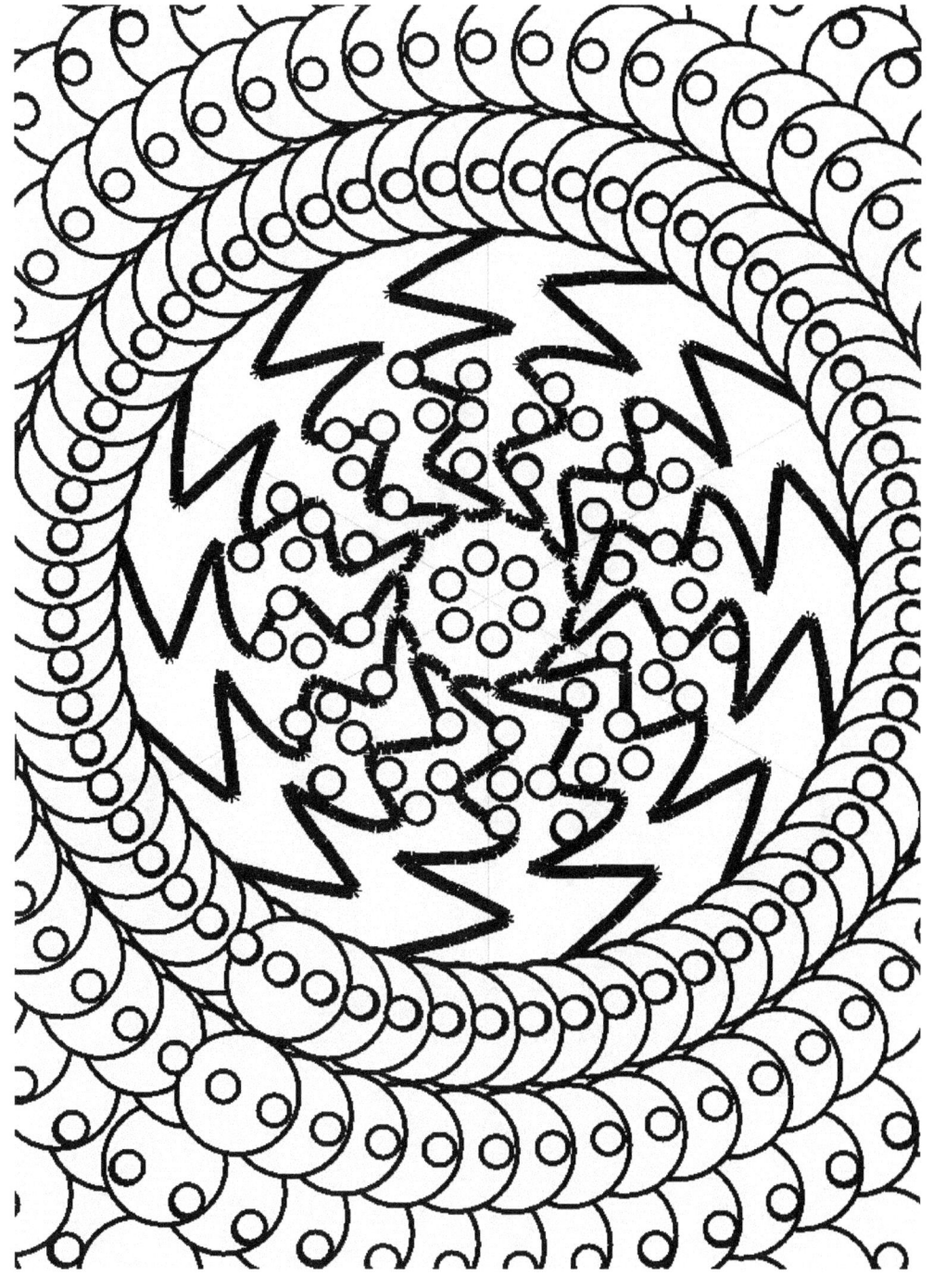

MAKE TODAY AMAZING

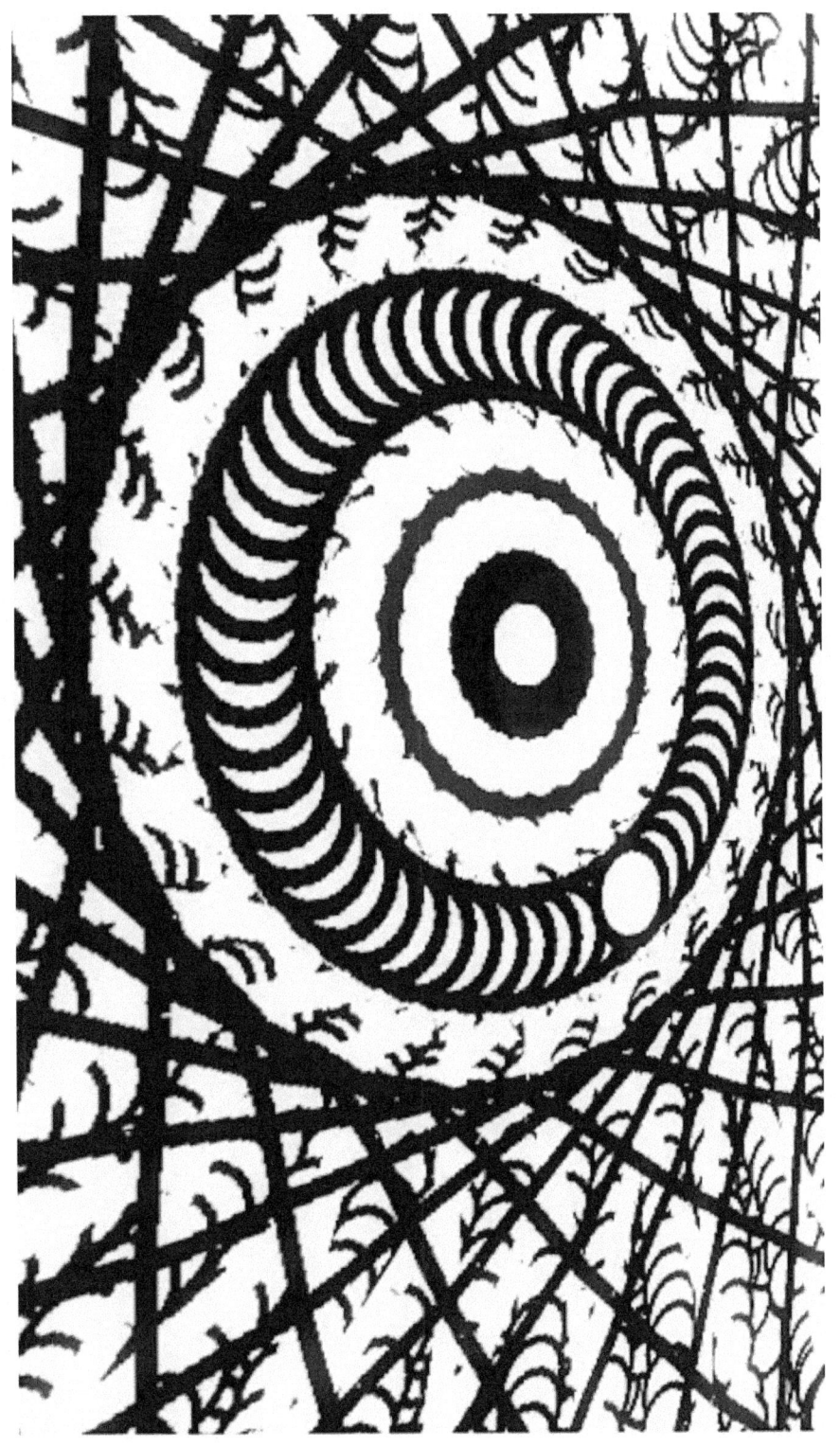

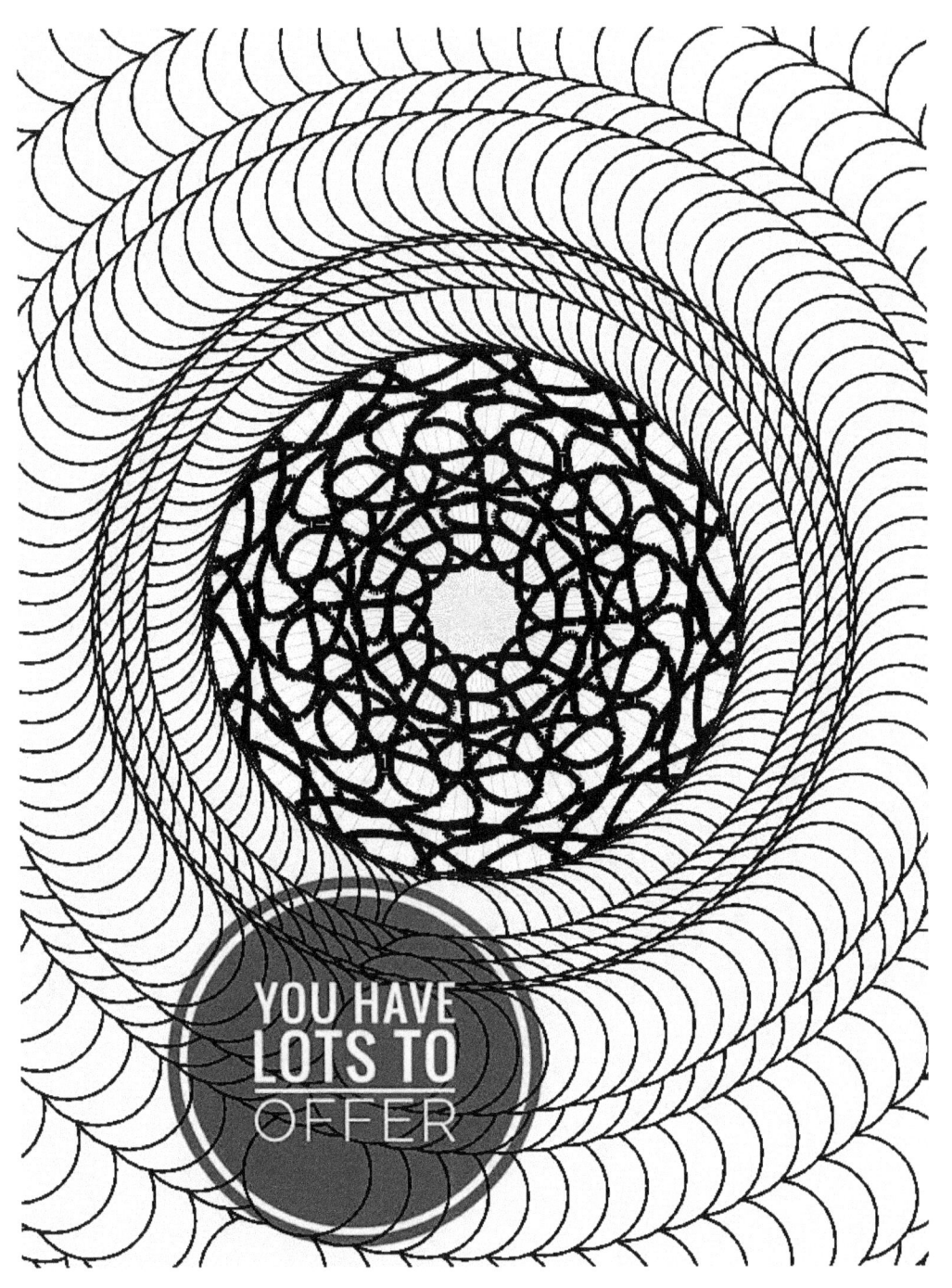

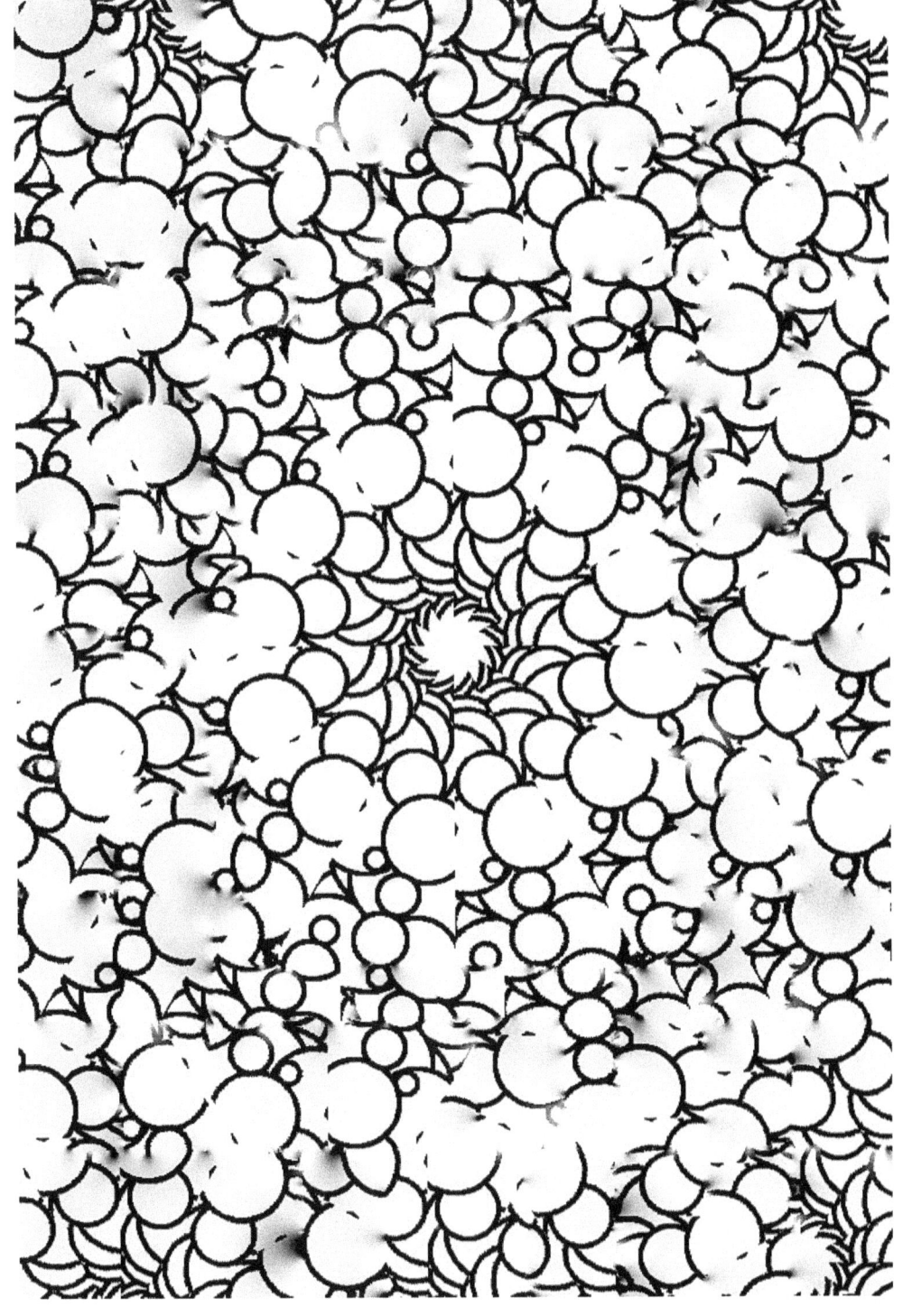

STAY WITH IT

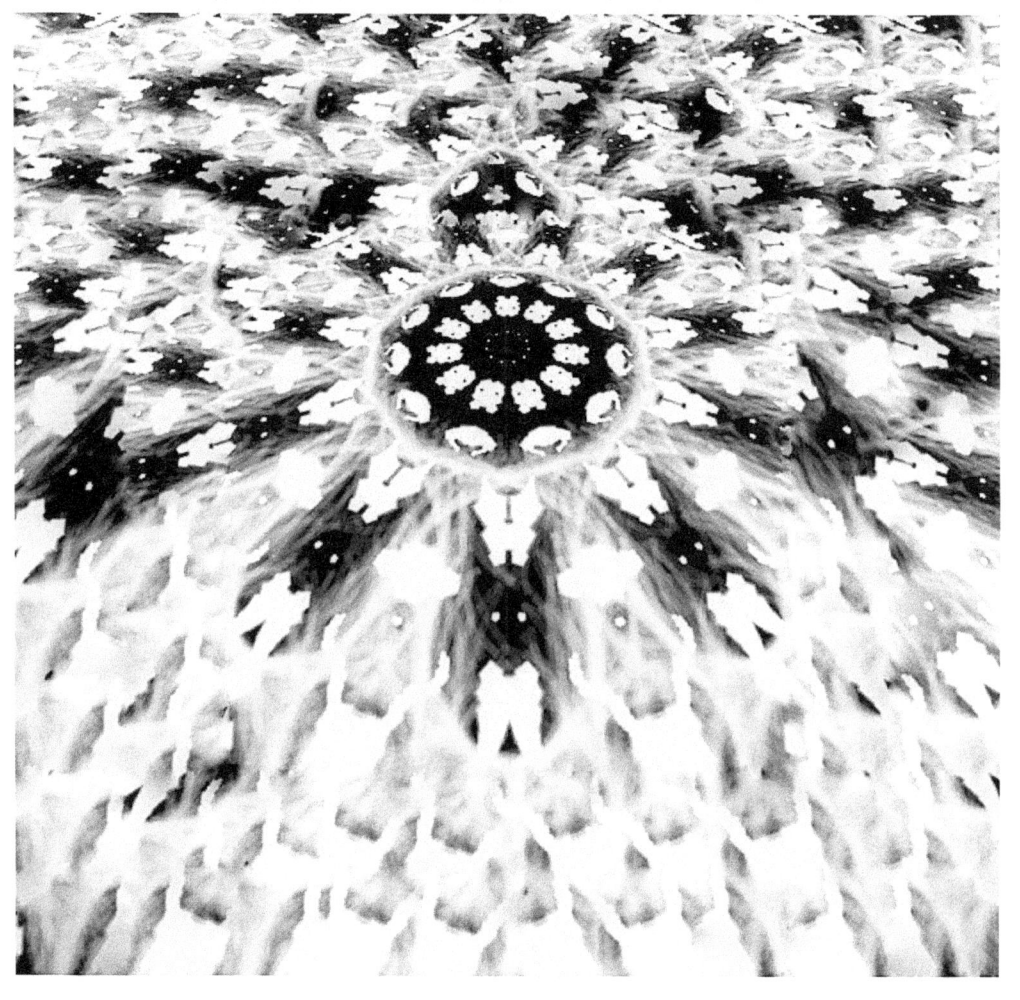

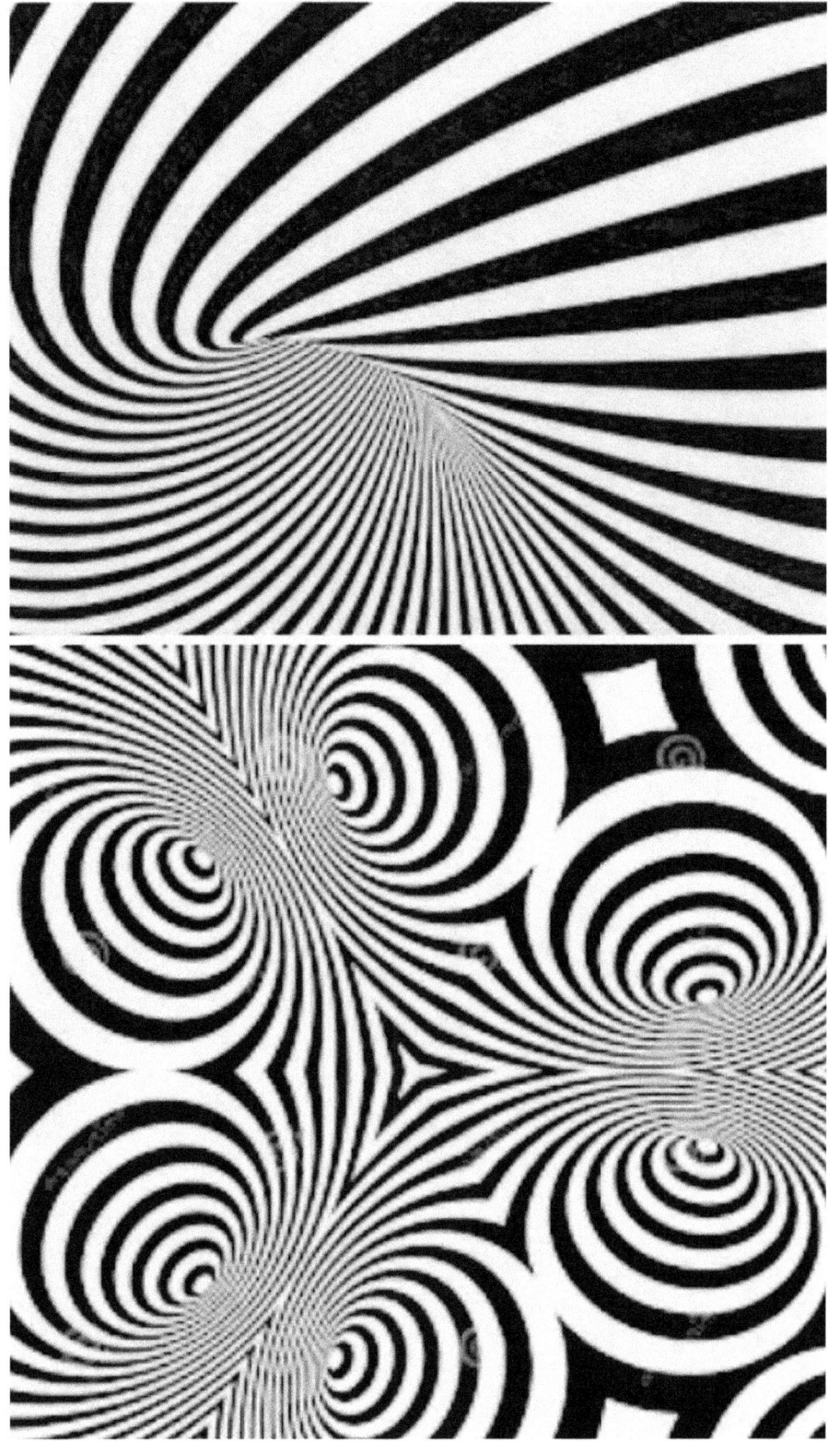

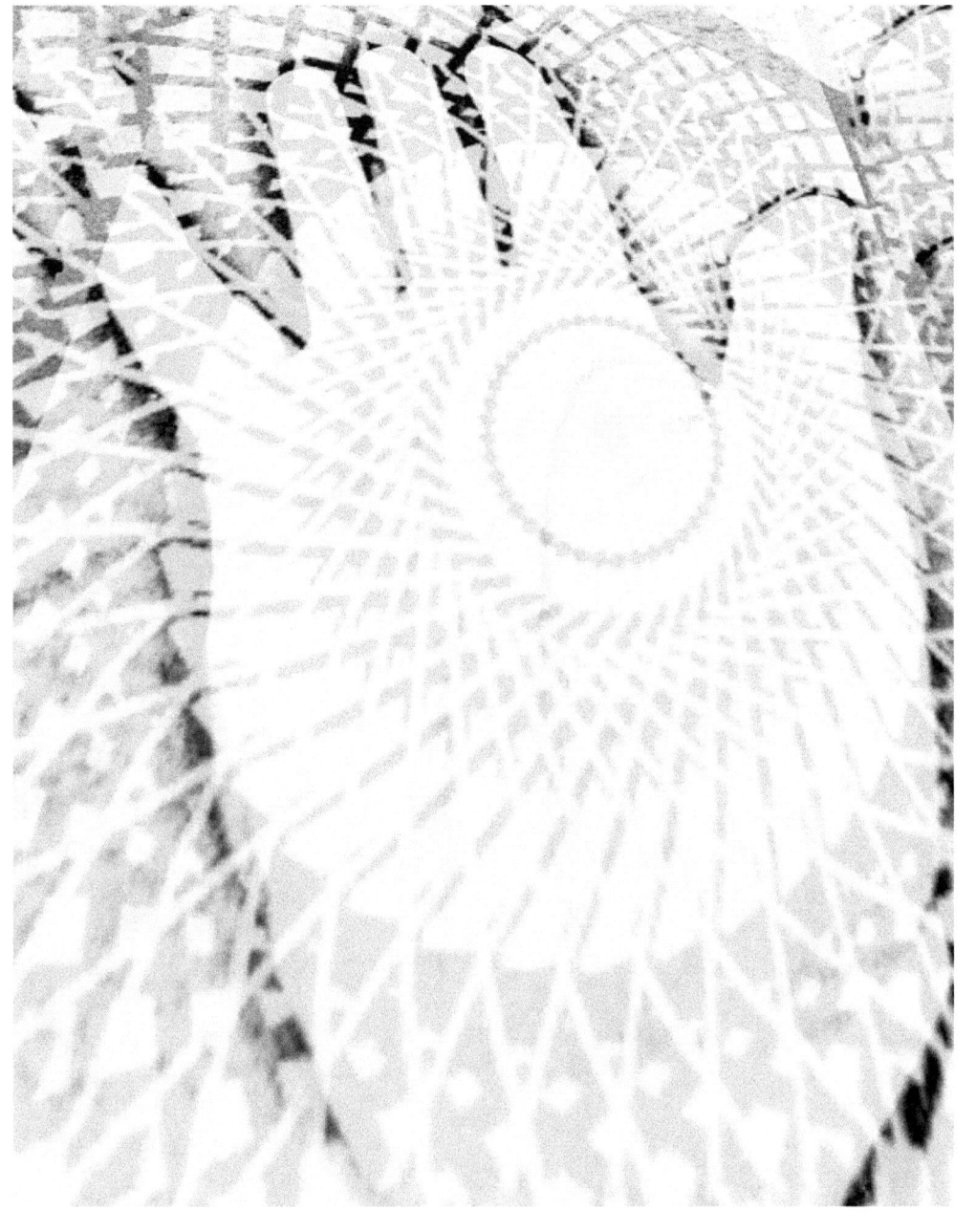

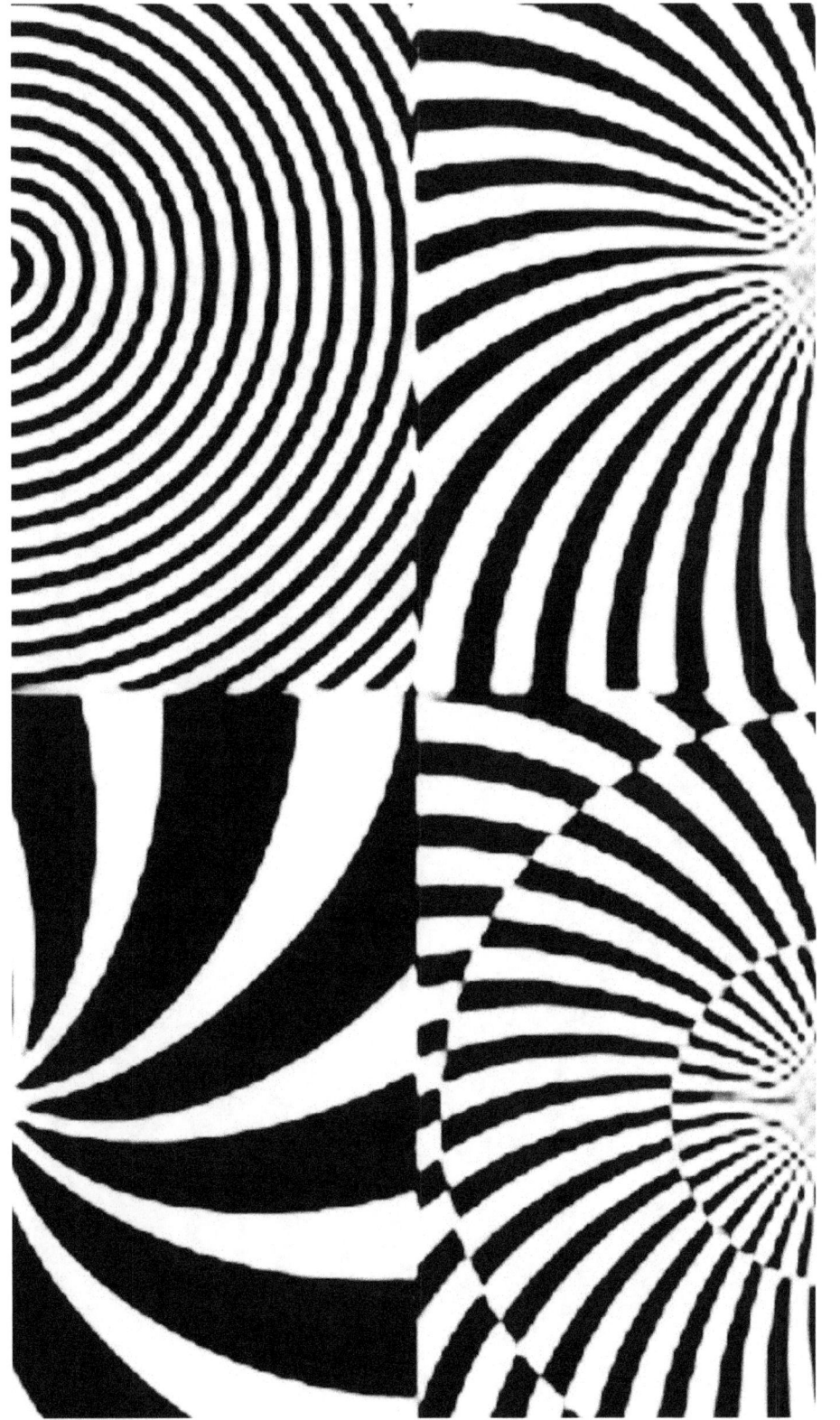

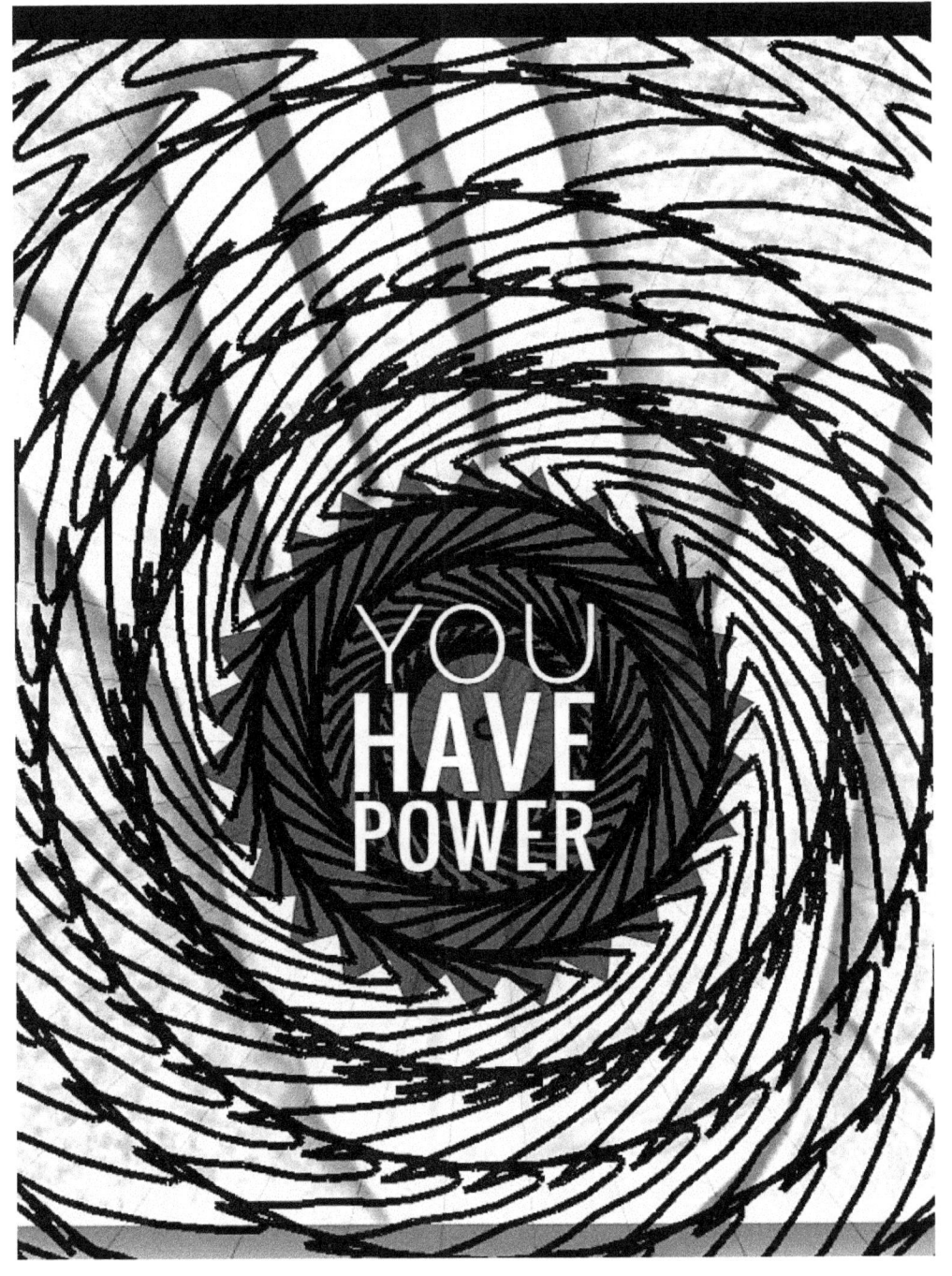

FORGIVE

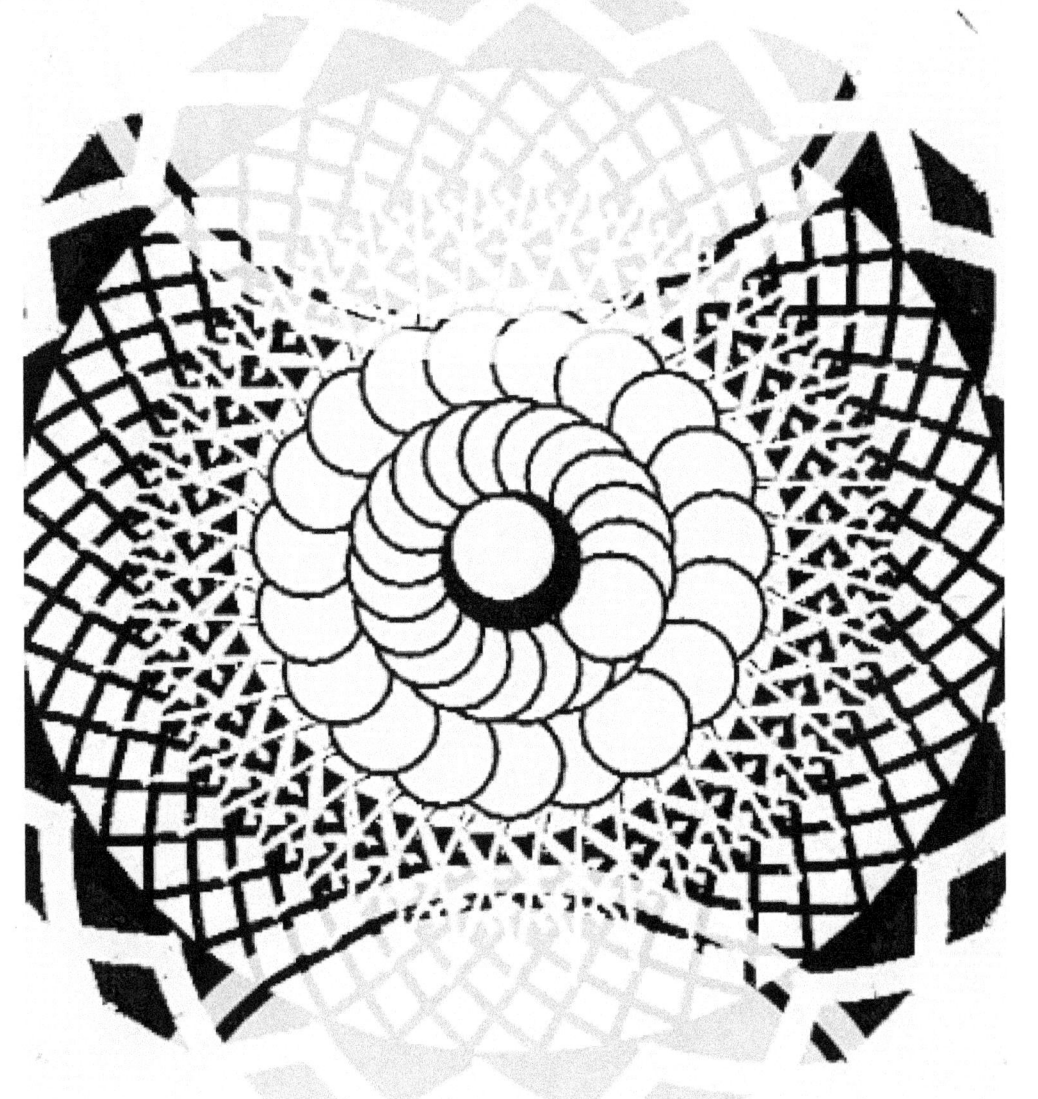

YOURSELF

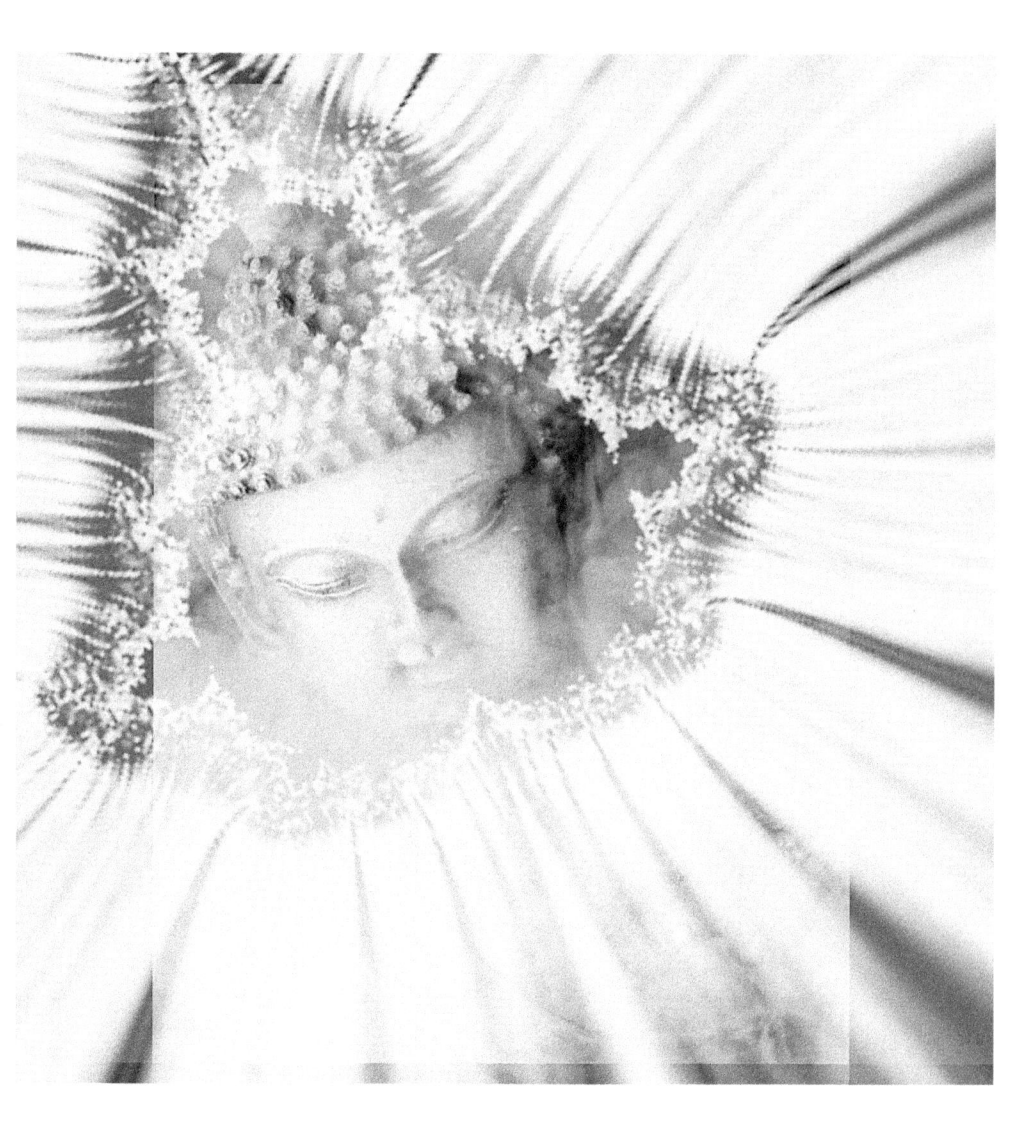

YOU ARE THE ONE

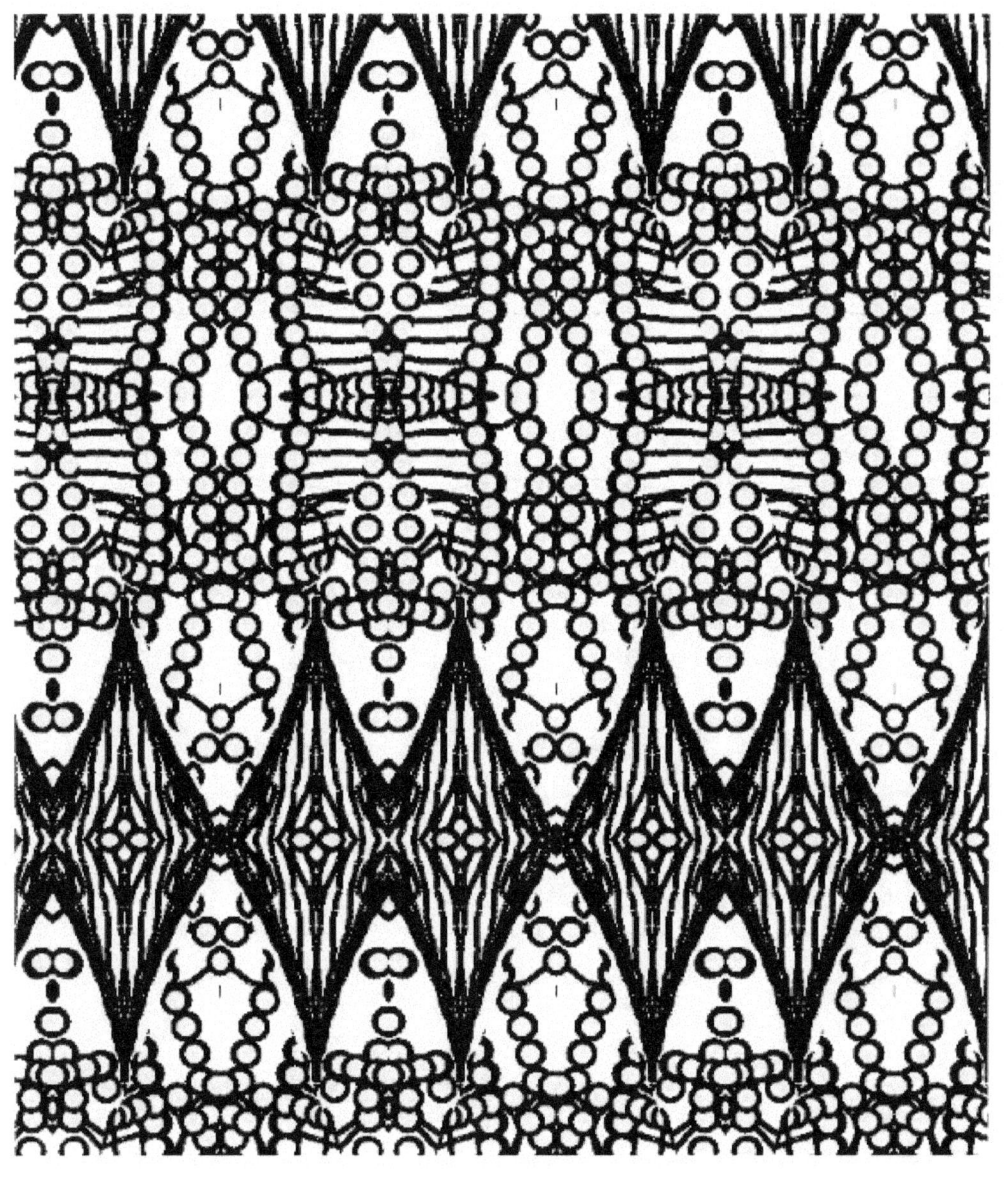

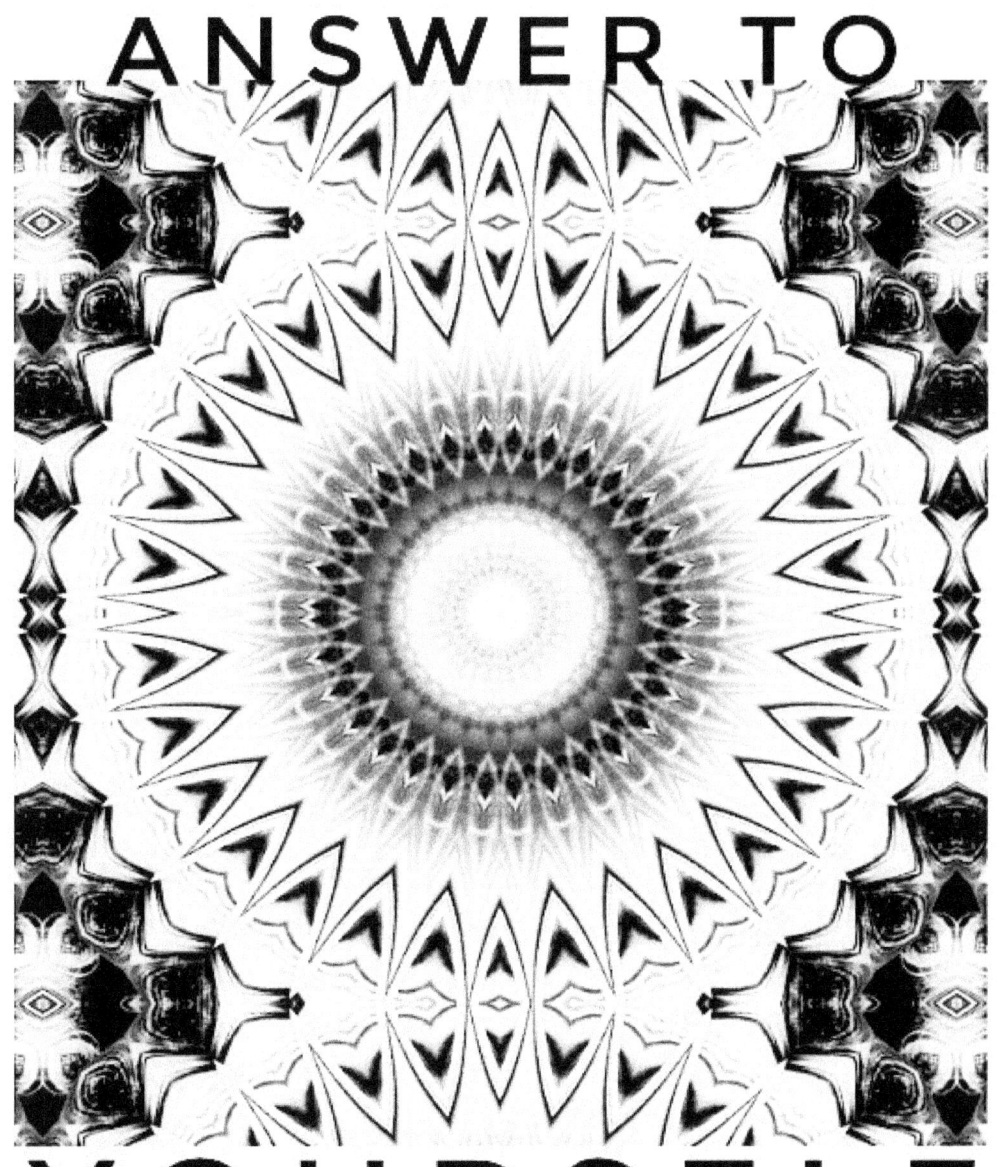

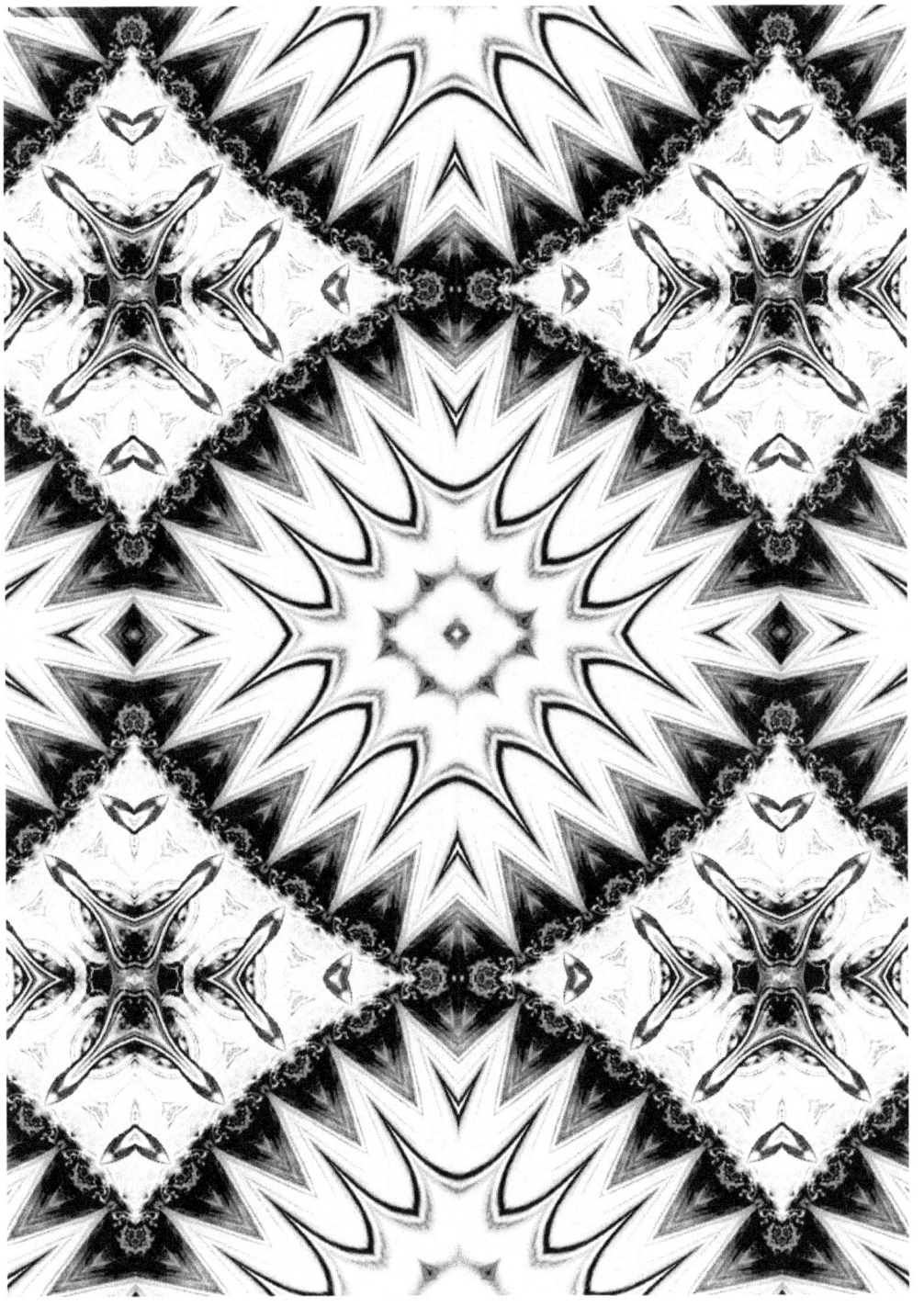

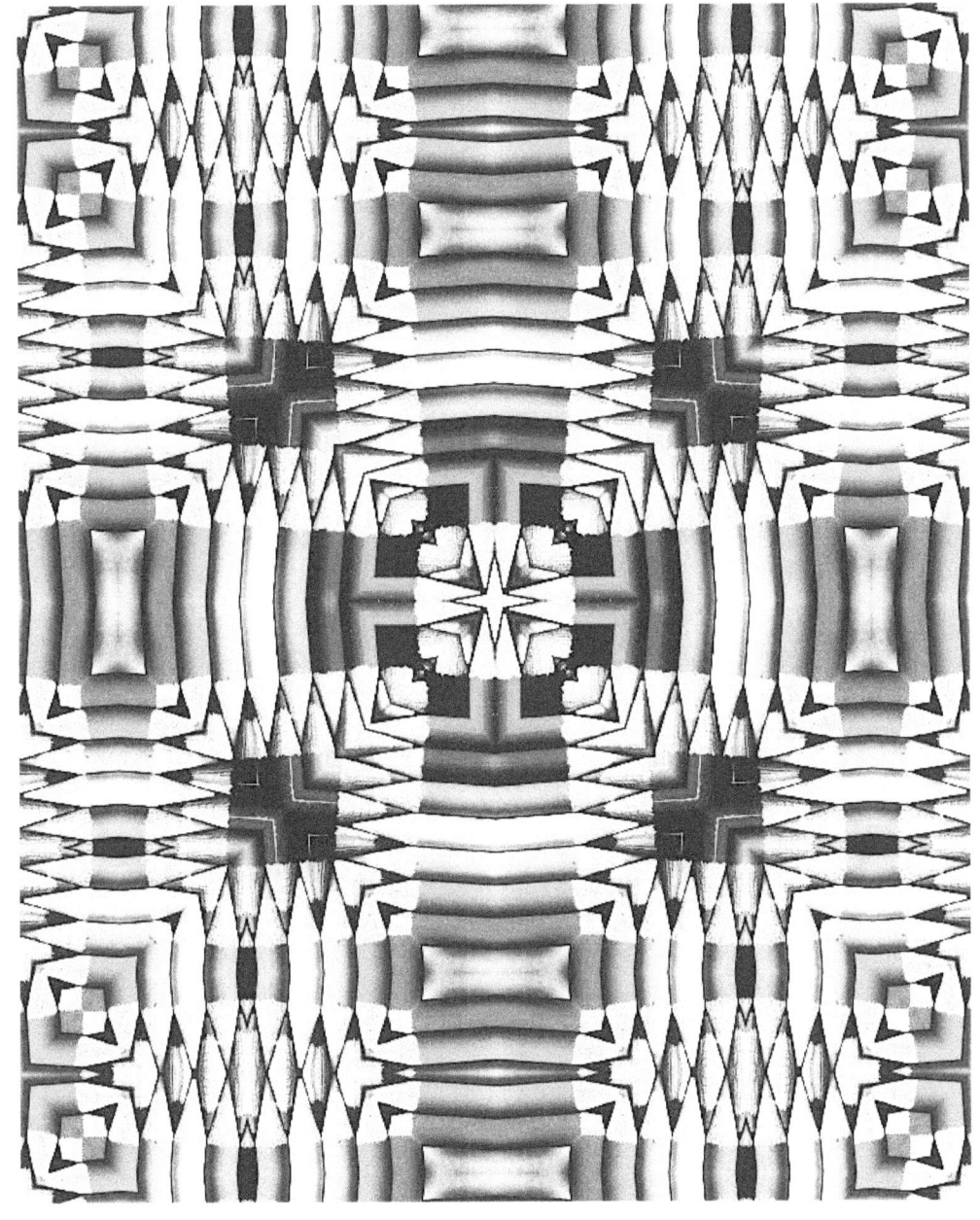

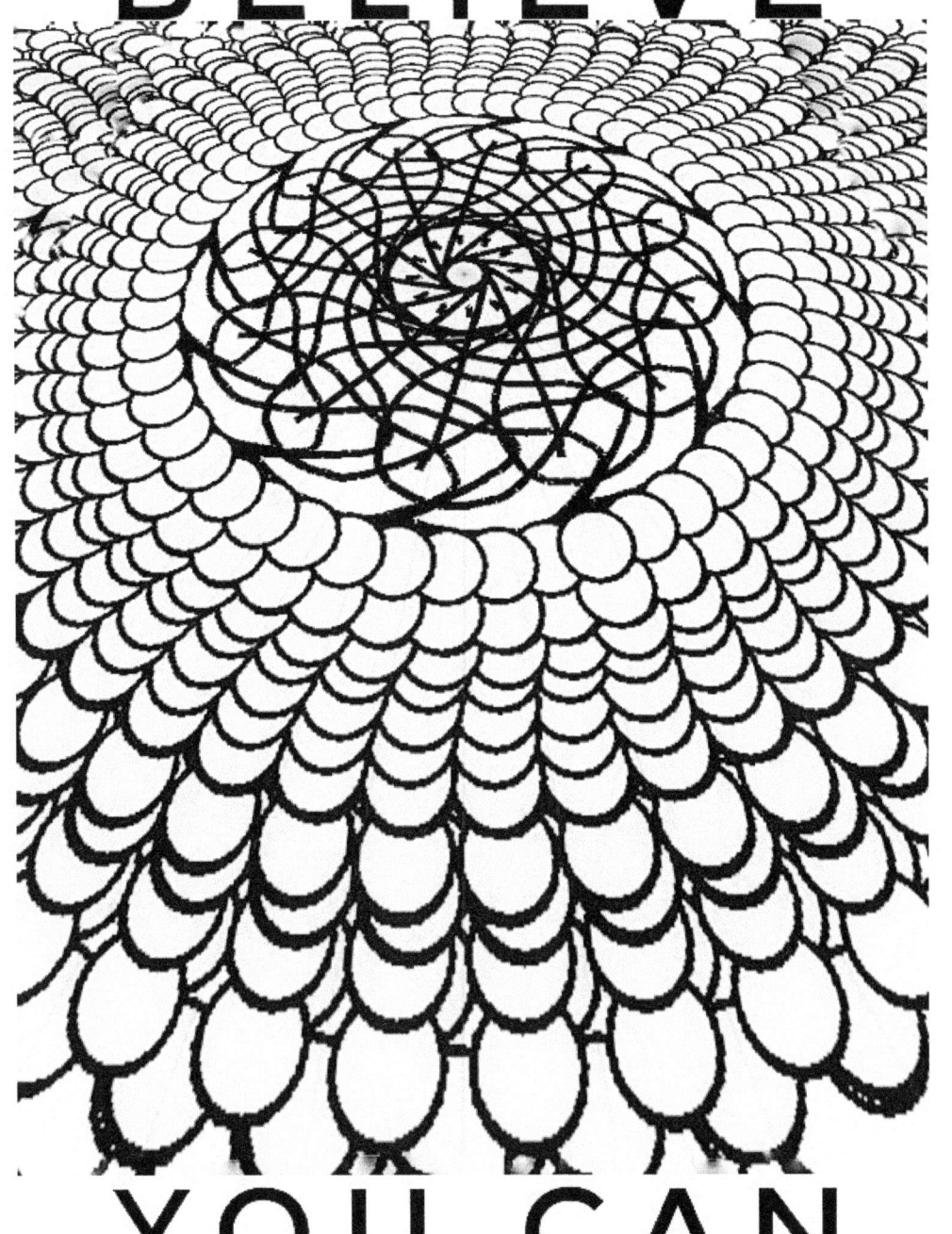

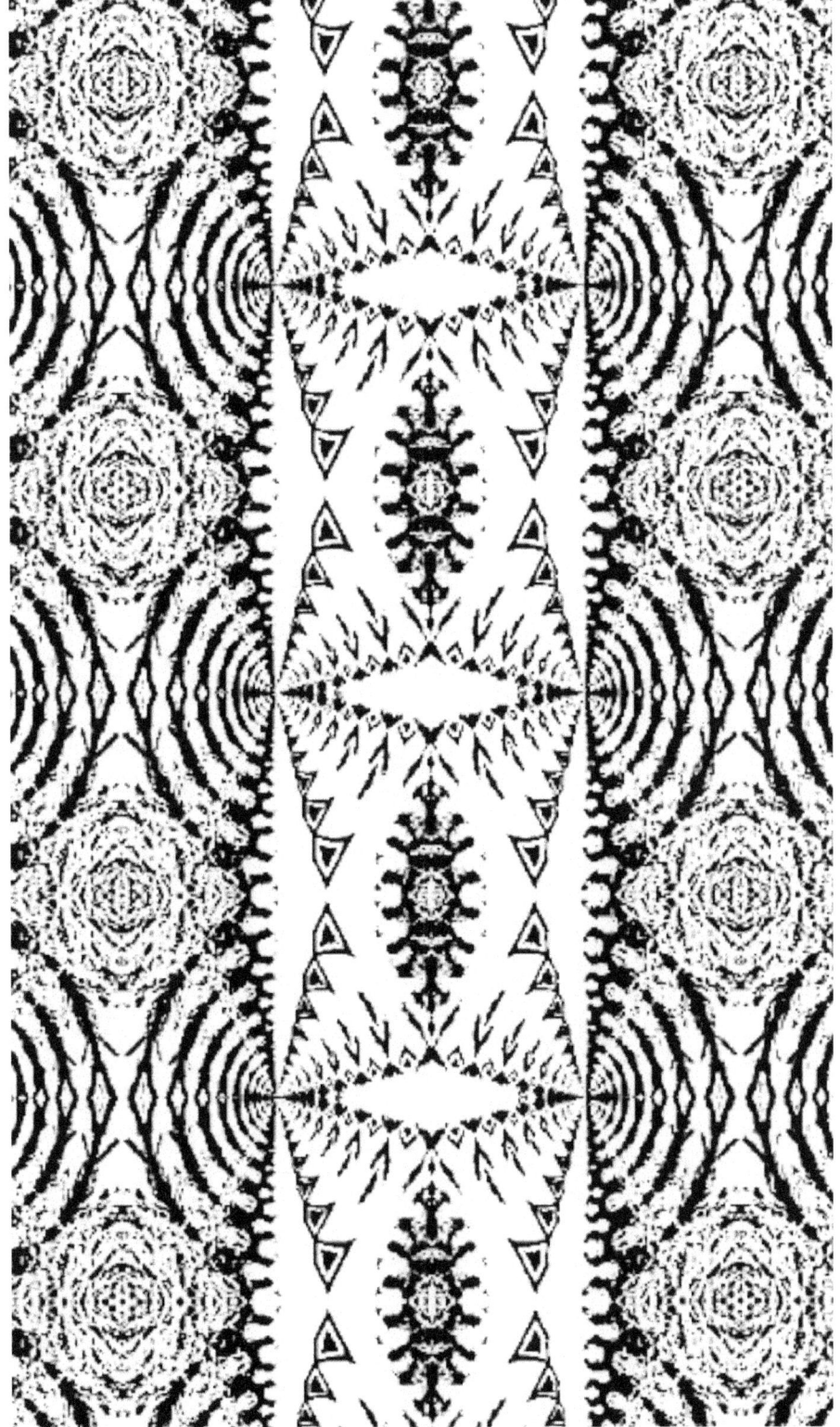

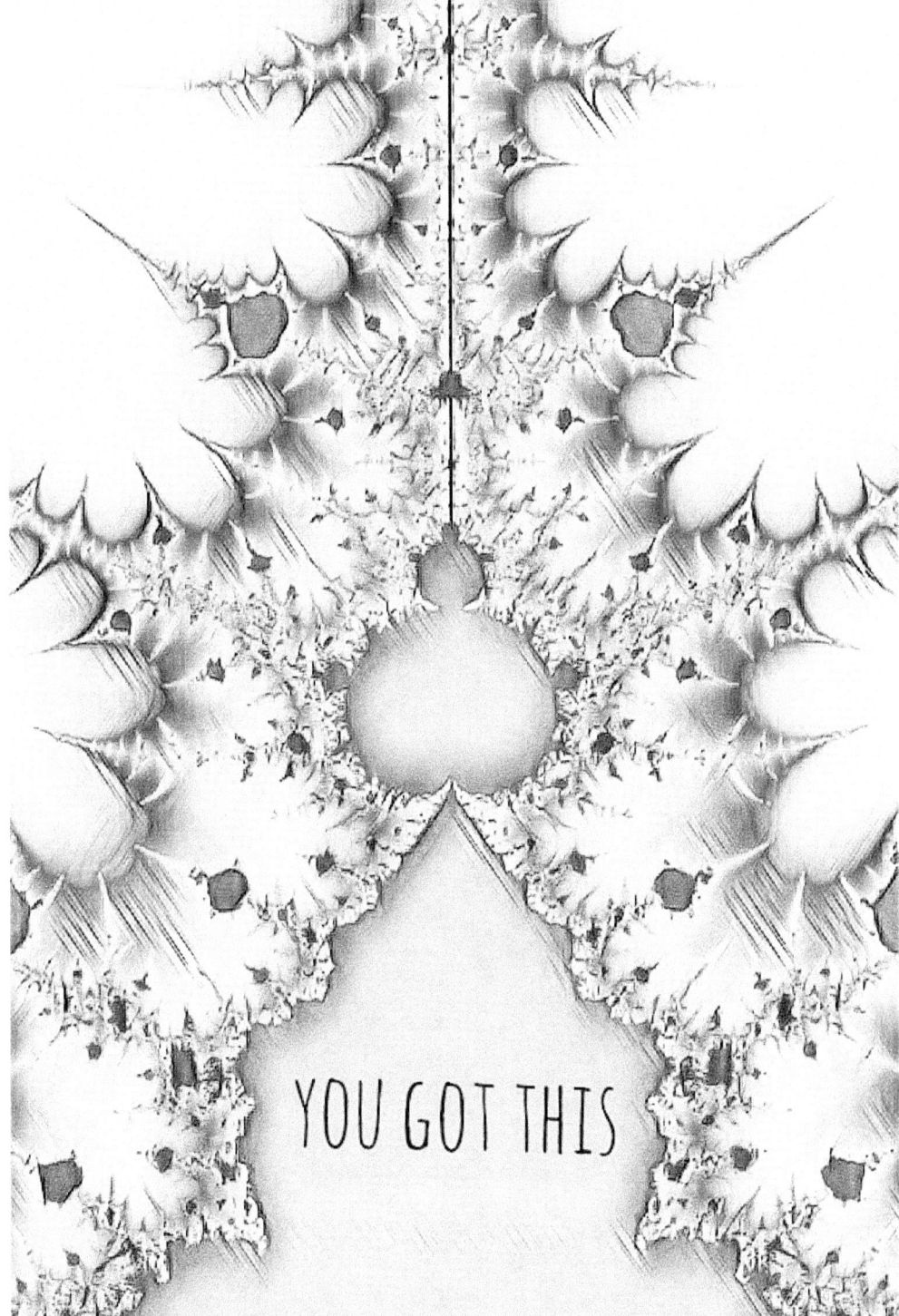

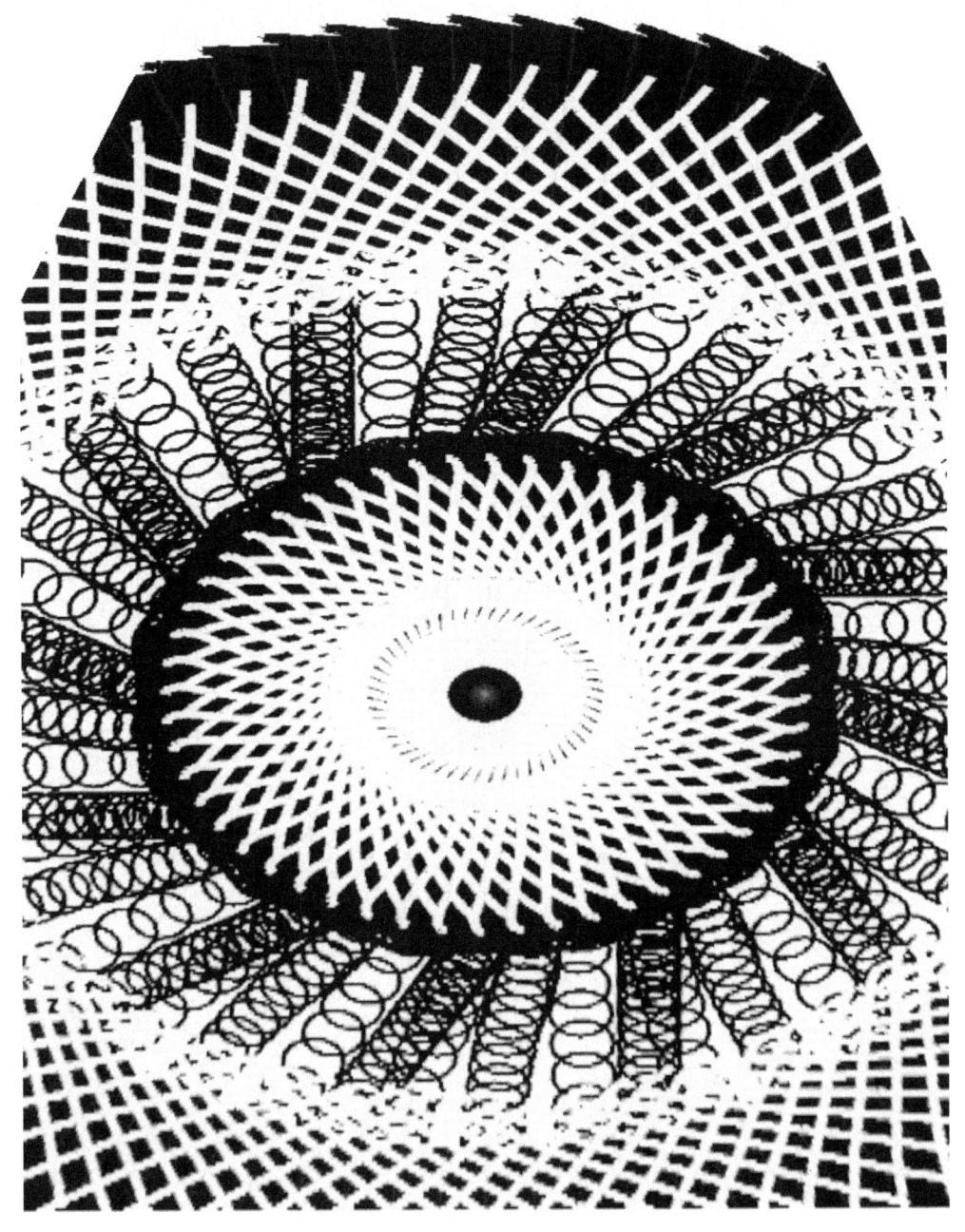

YOU HAVE A LOT

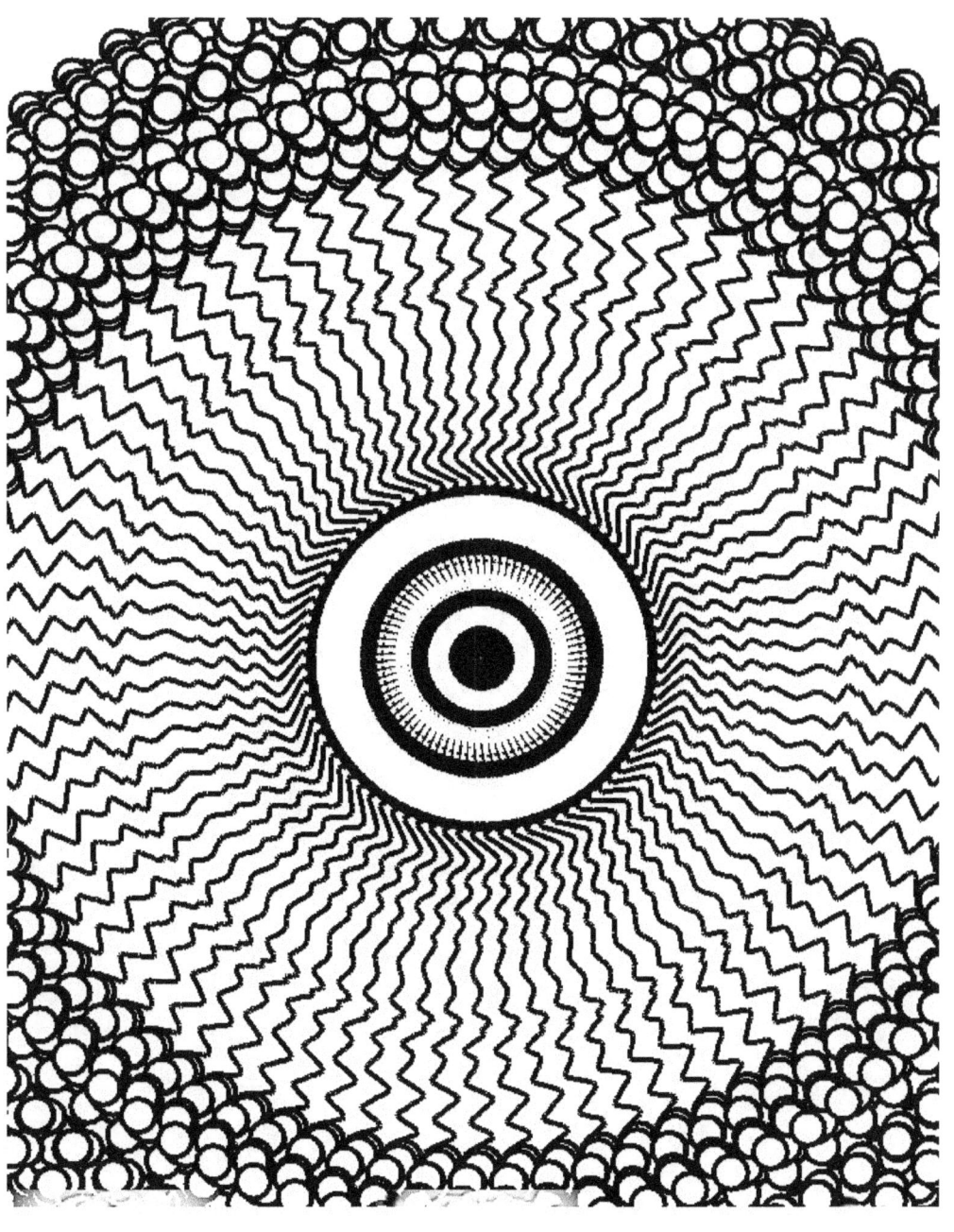

GOING FOR YOU

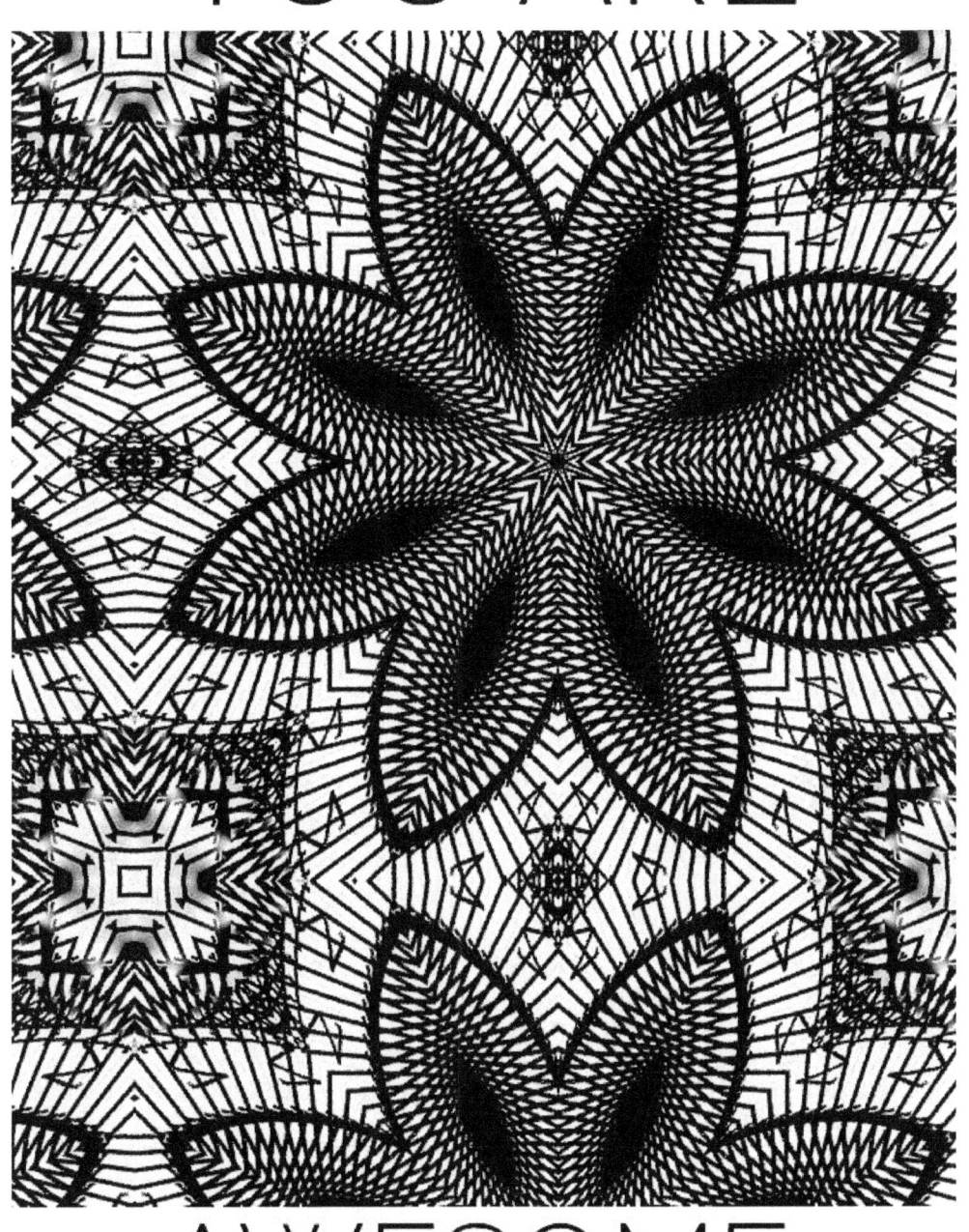

YOU ARE AWESOME

IMPRESS

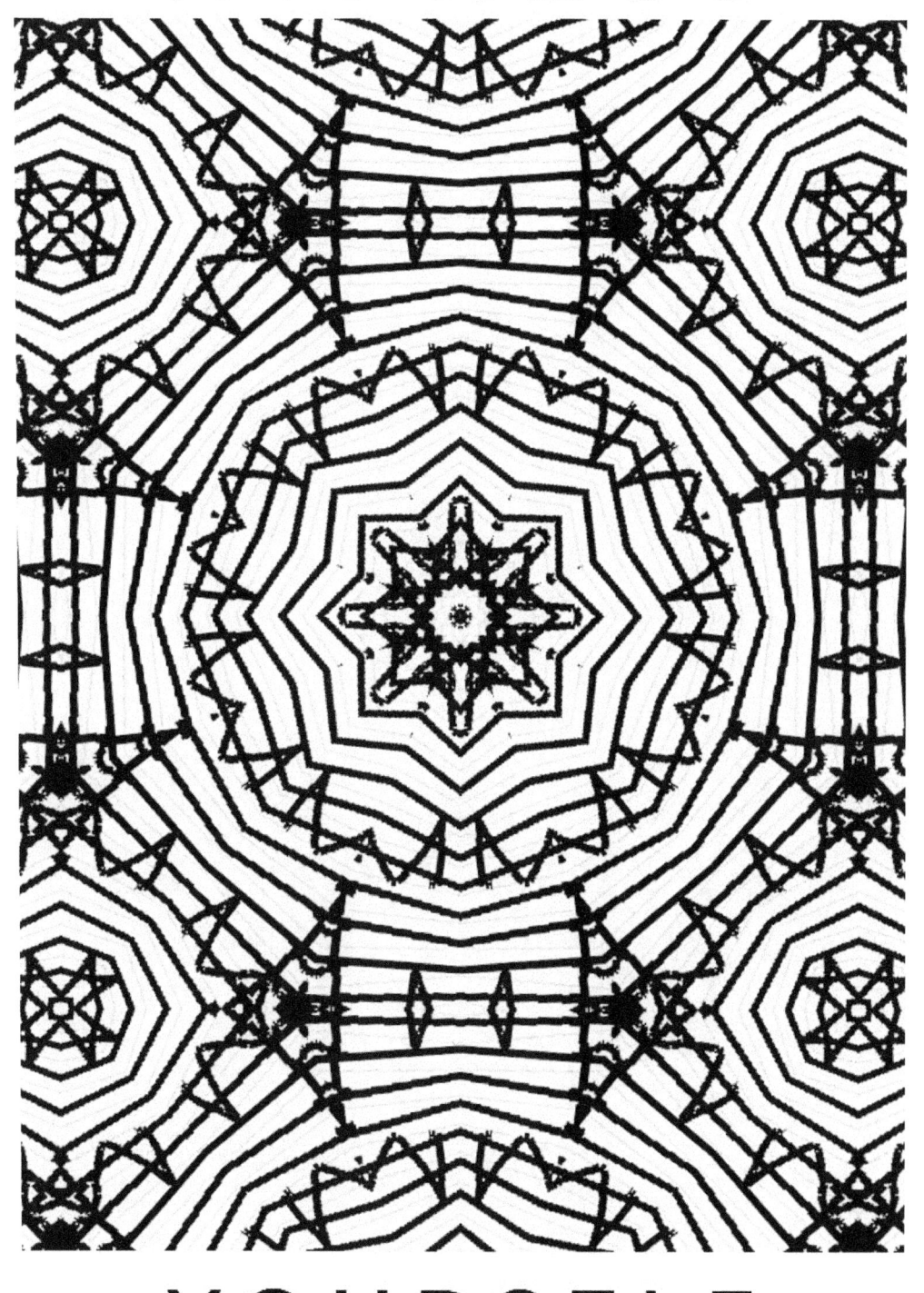

YOURSELF

BELIEVE

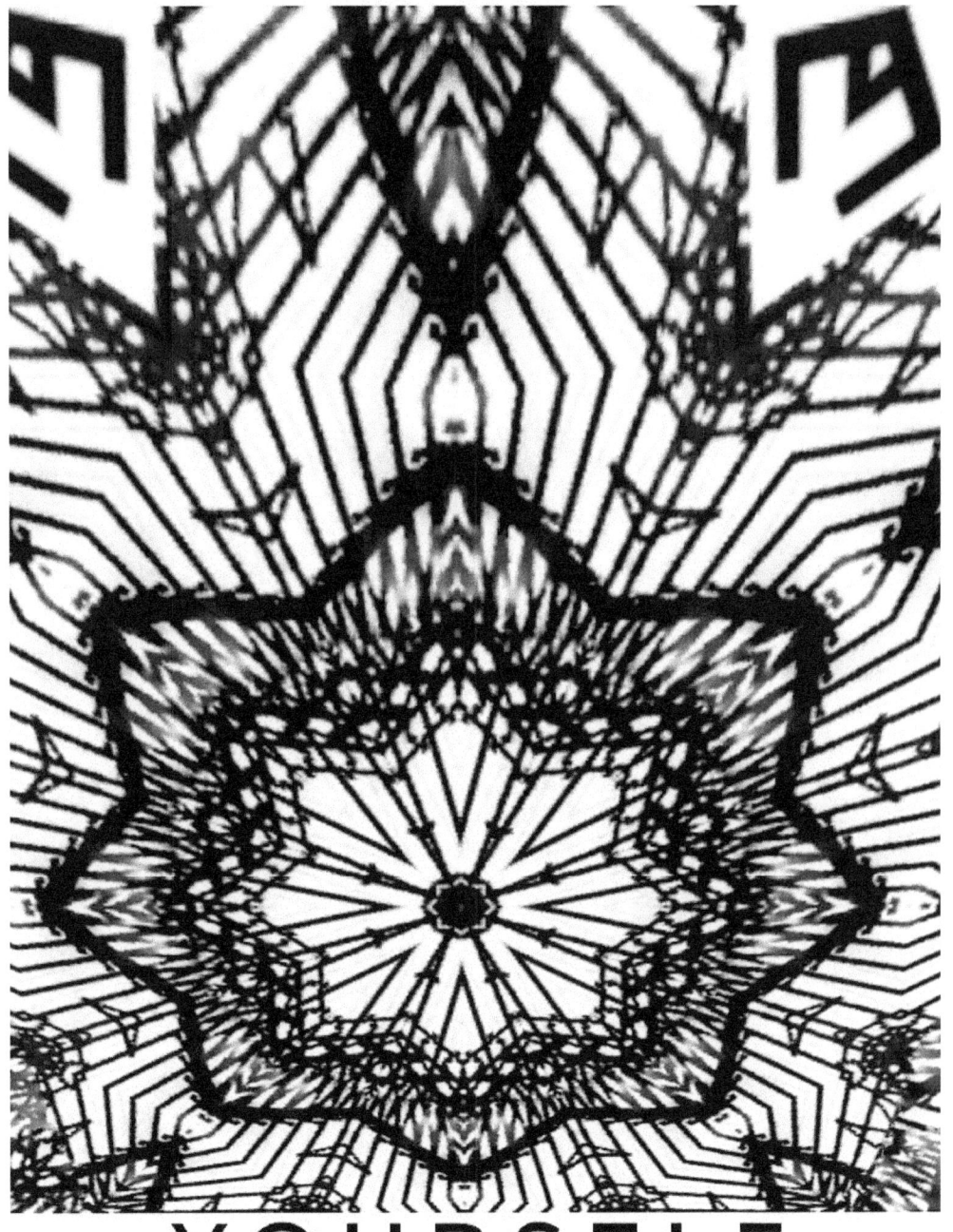

YOURSELF

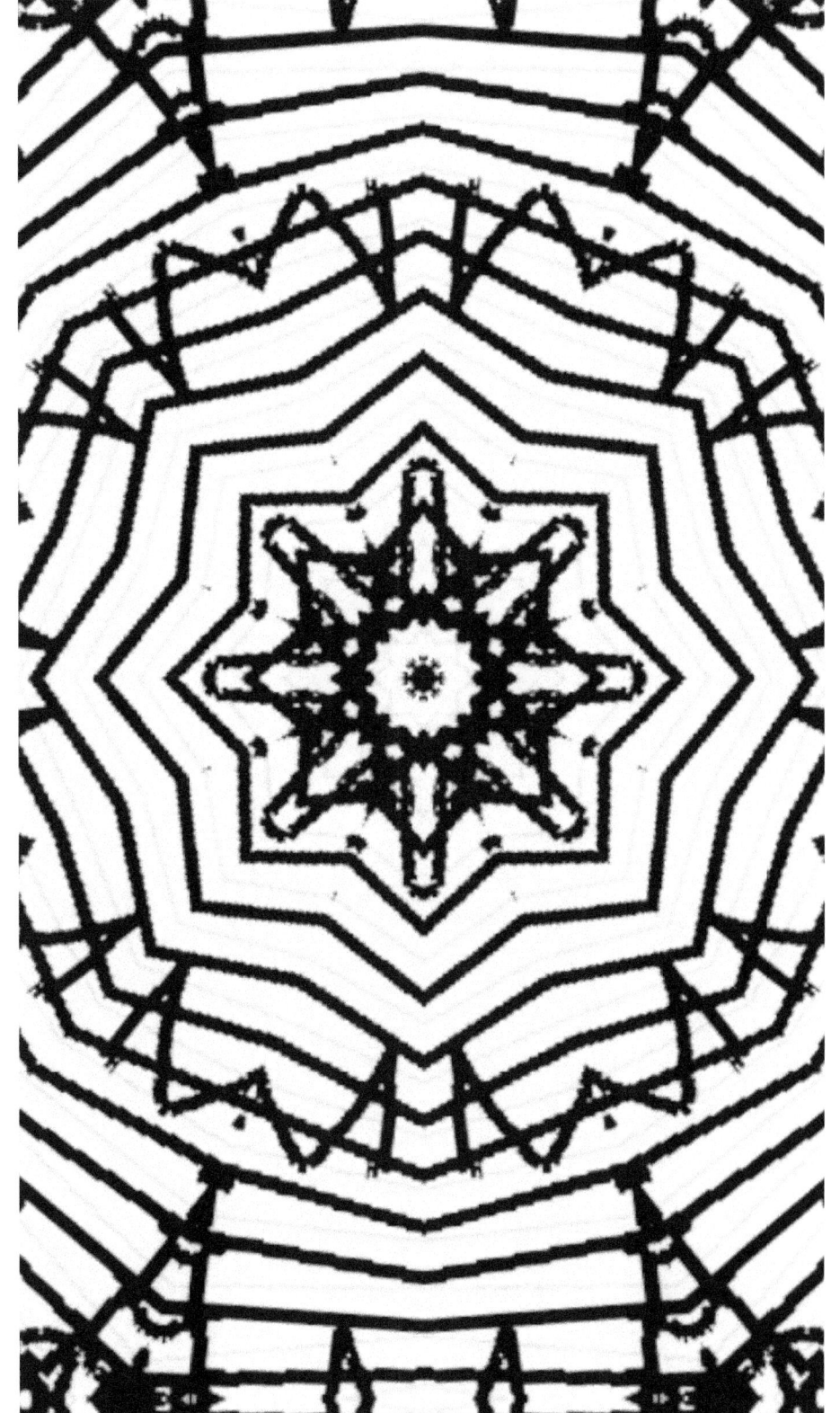

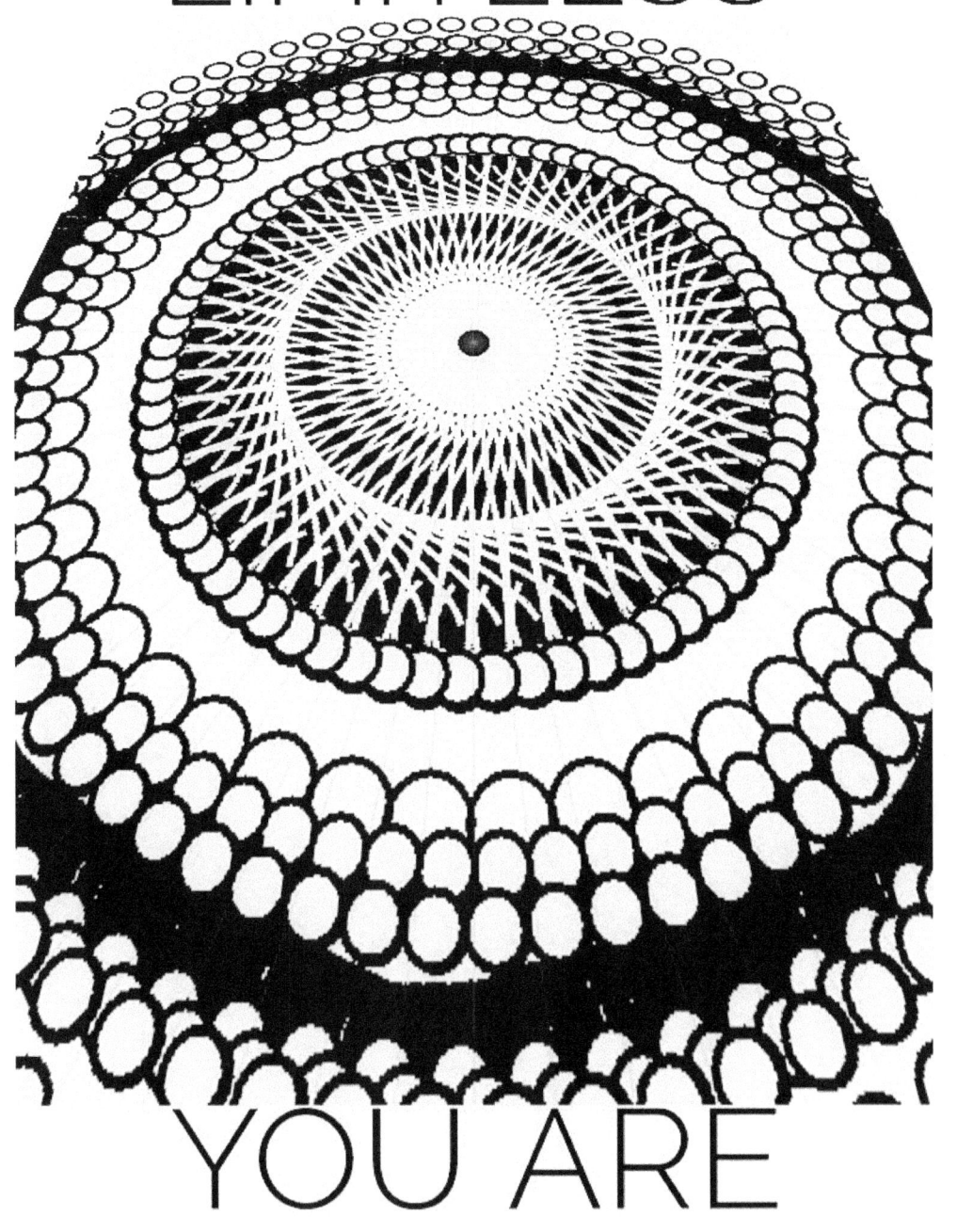

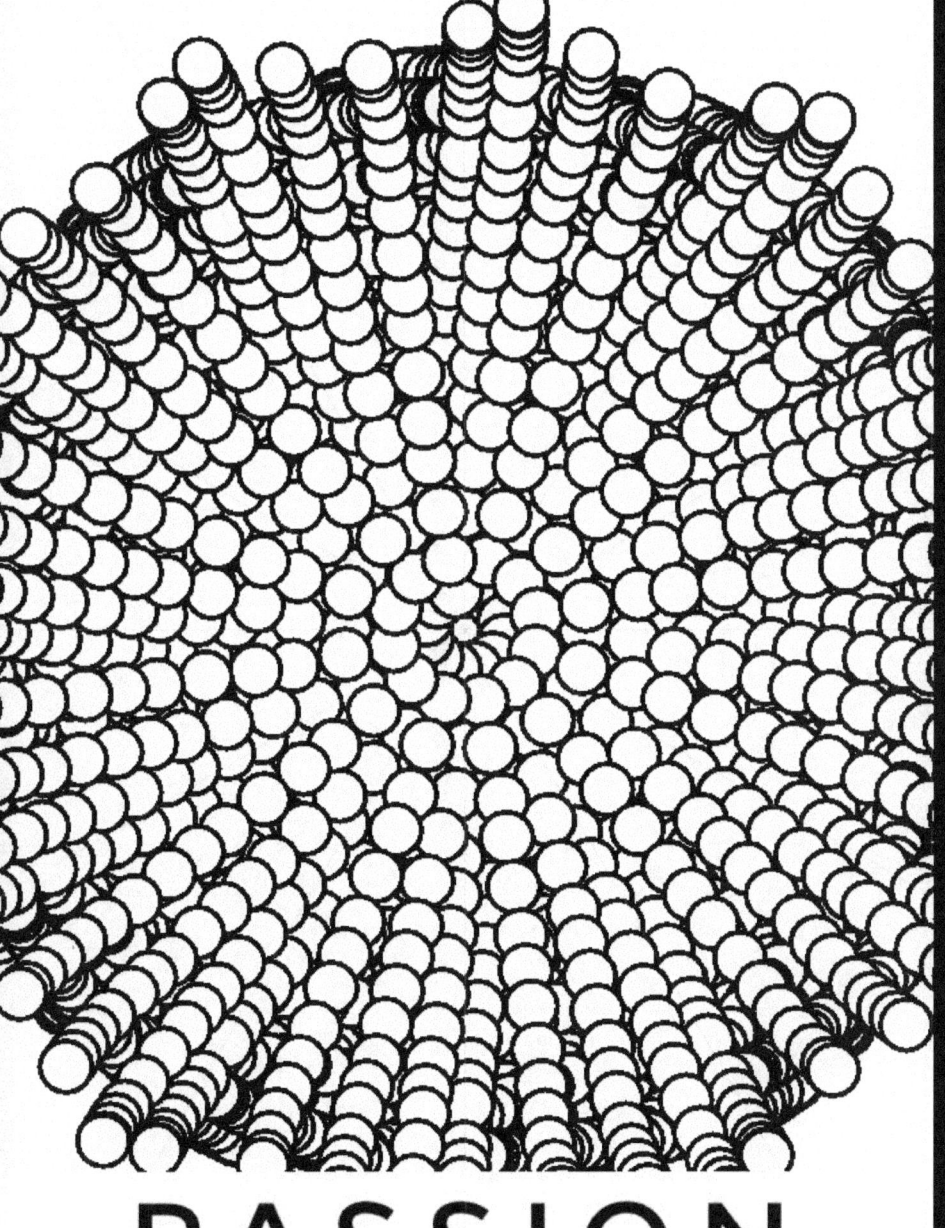

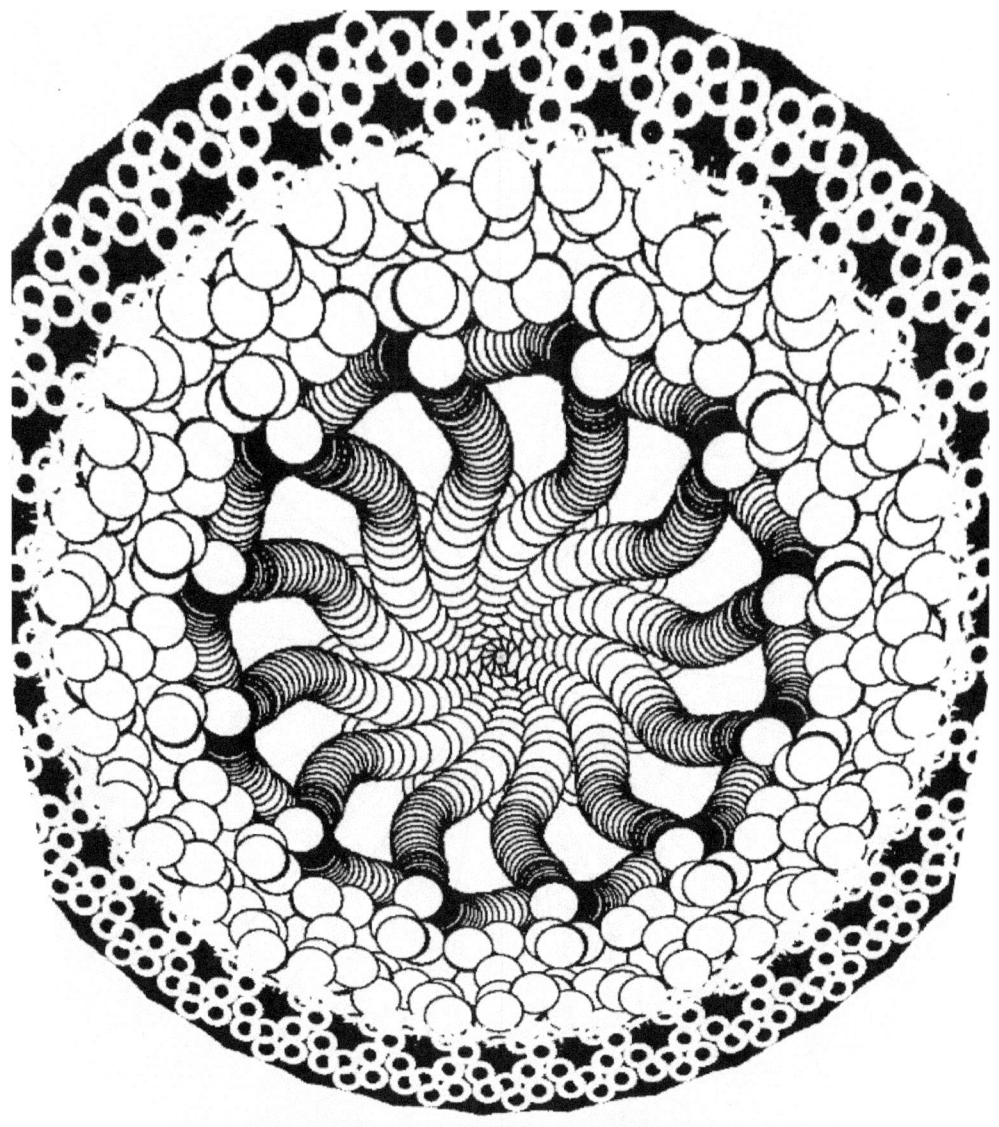

LIFE IS

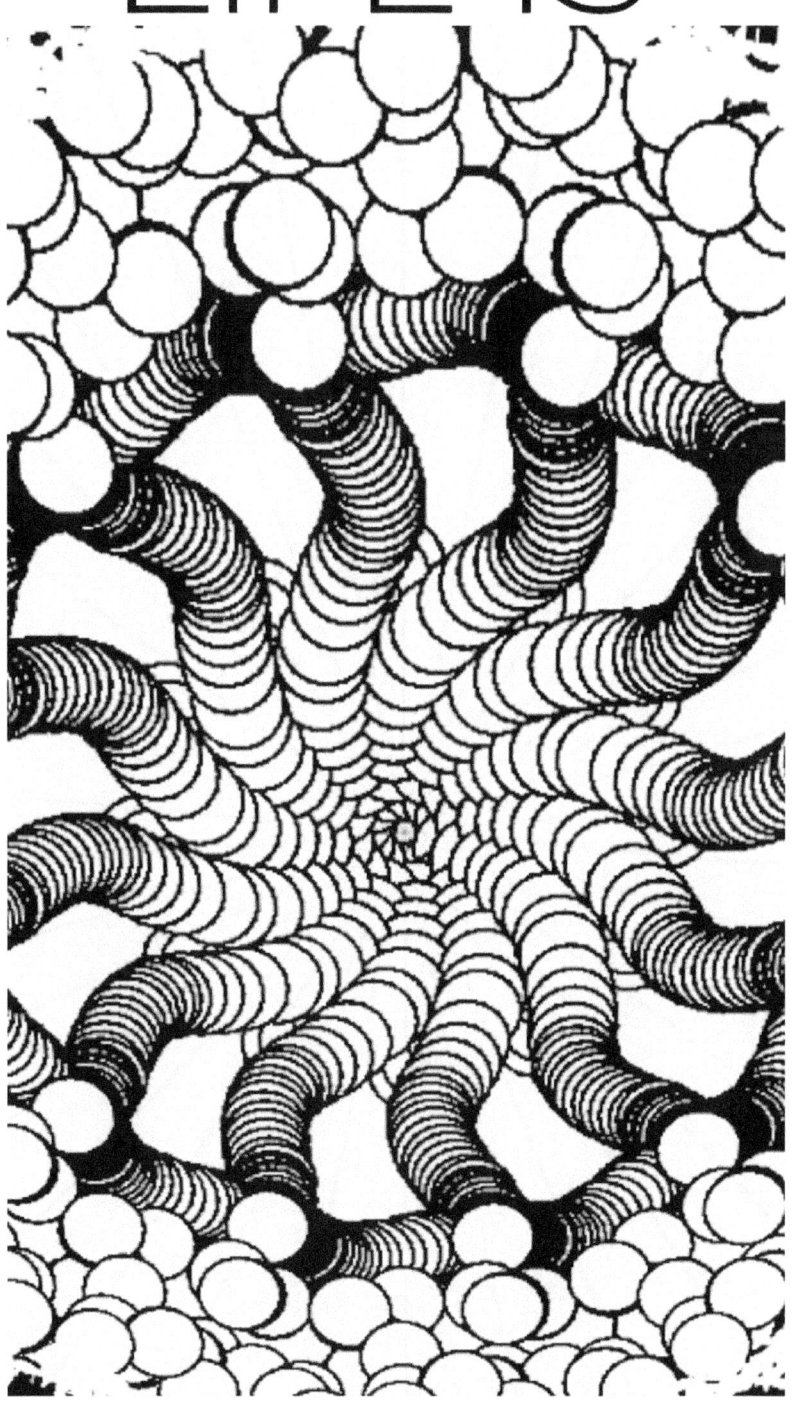

ADVENTURE

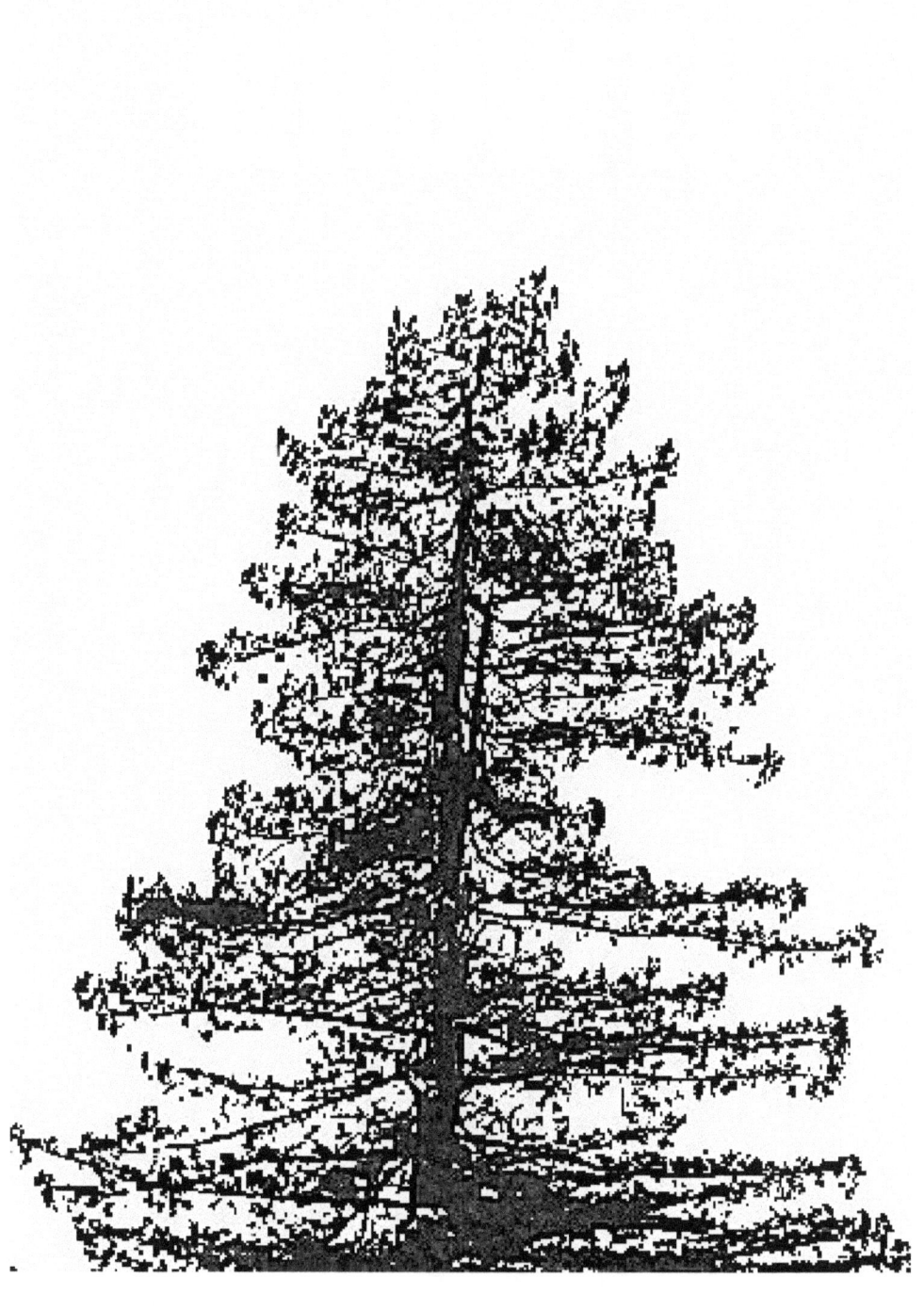

YOUR OBSTACLES

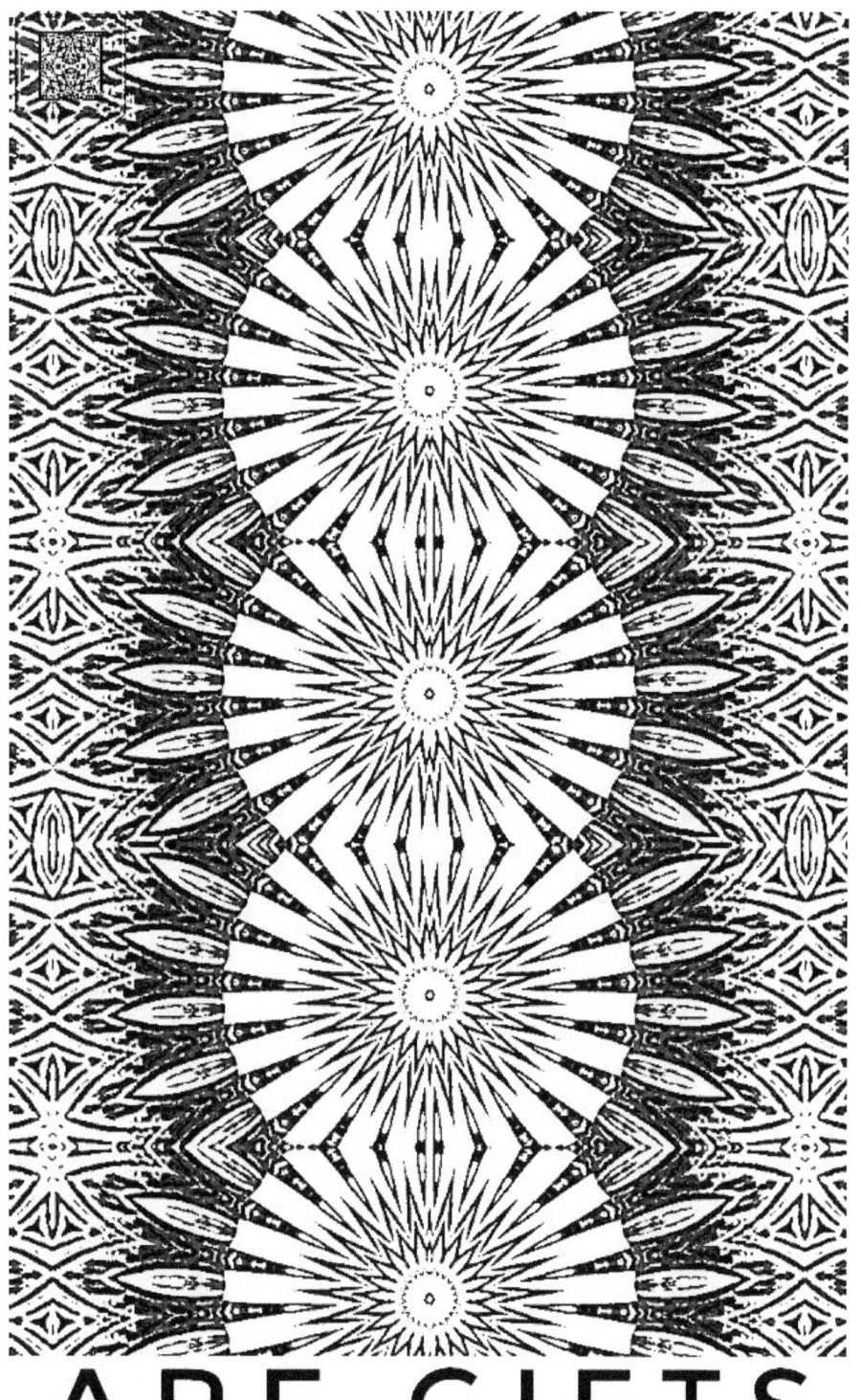

ARE GIFTS

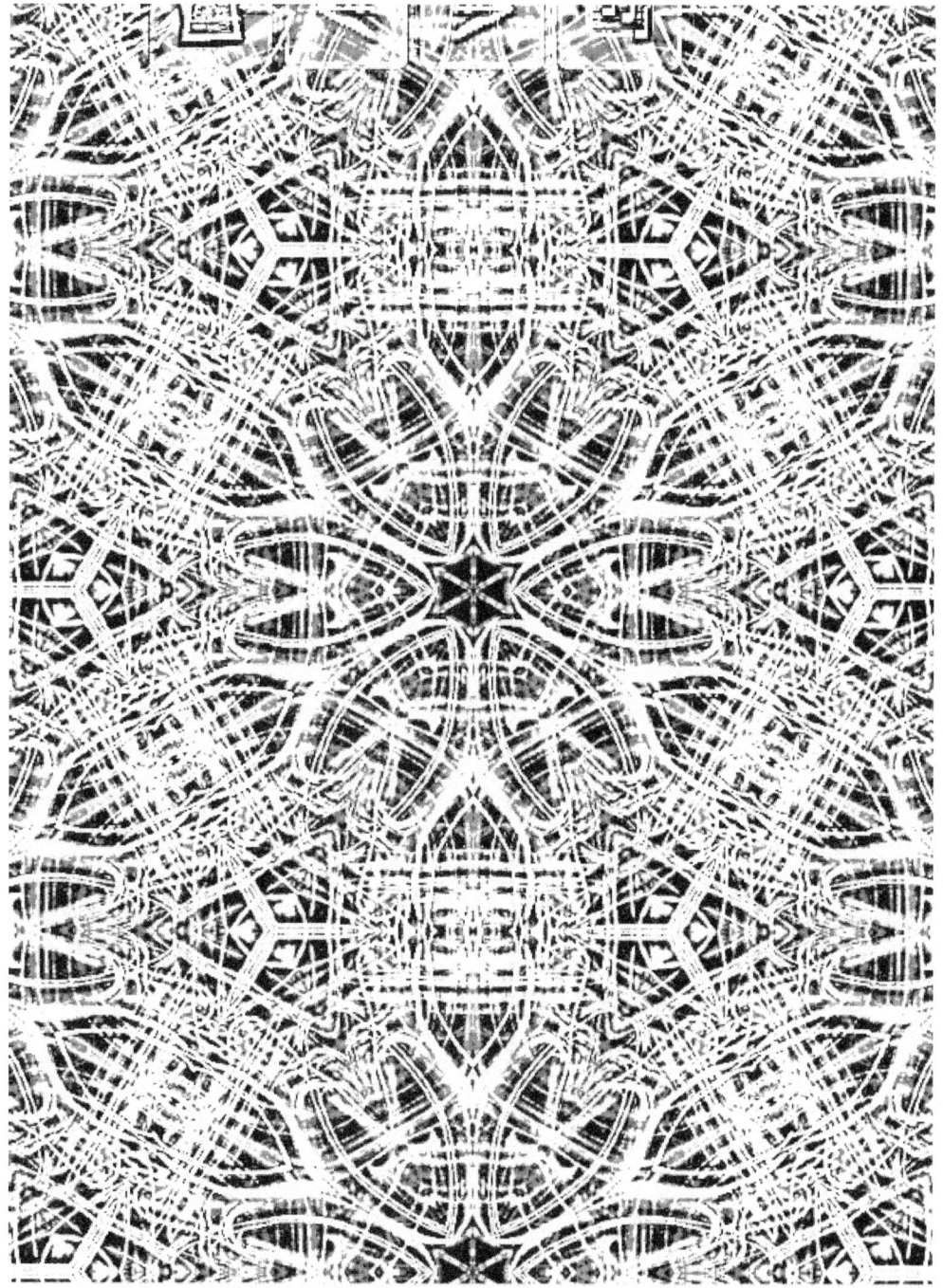

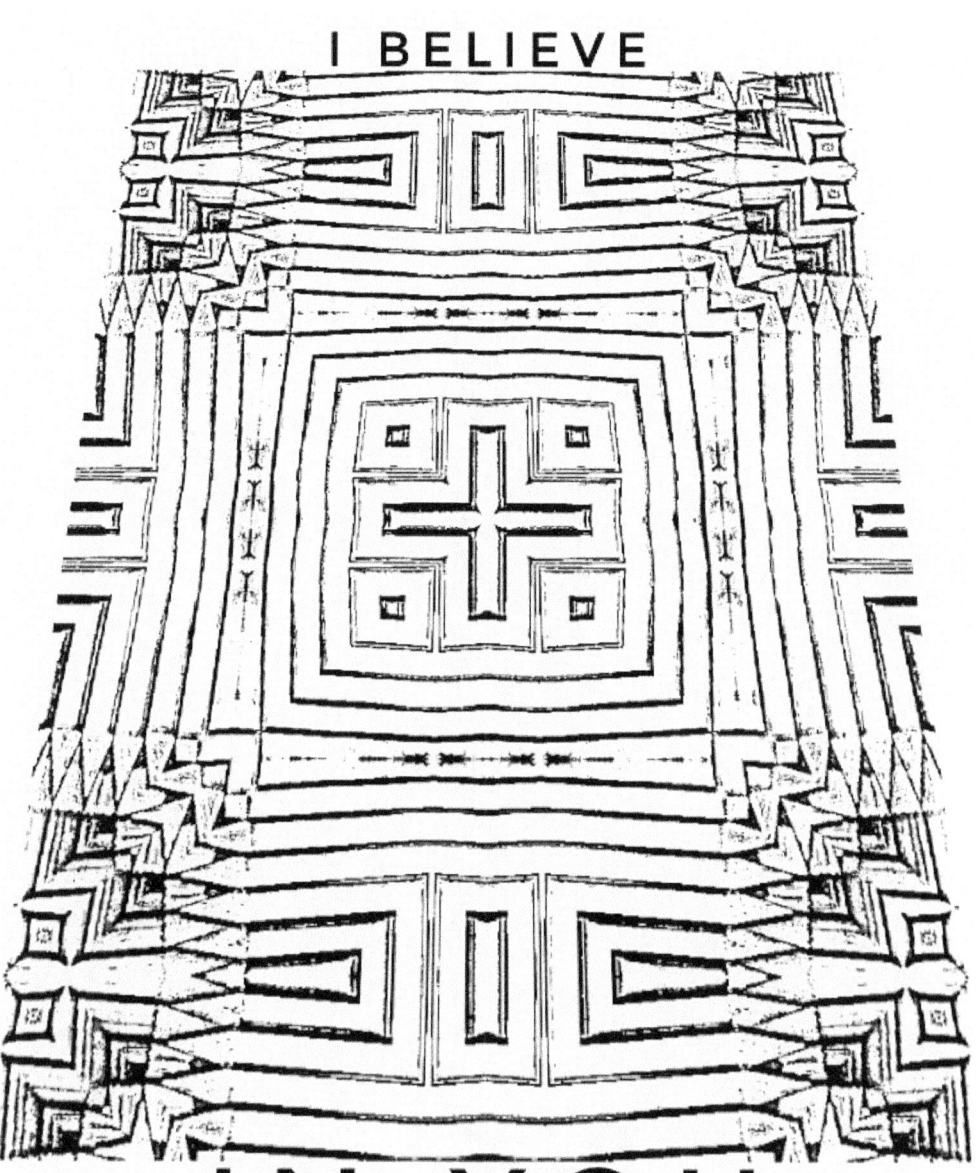

www.ingramcontent.com/pod-product-compliance
Lightning Source LLC
Chambersburg PA
CBHW070157230526
45471CB00002B/709